FABIO CAMPOLI
La mia Cucina 100 RECIPES

©2014
Autentica Srl
Via Due Giugno, 25
00019 Tivoli (Roma)

@2014
Il Circolo dei Buongustai di Fabio Campoli
Via Tenuta del Cavaliere, 1
00012 Guidonia Montecelio (Roma)
www.fabiocampoli.it
www.ilcircolodeibuongustai.net

Contents
Fabio Campoli

Editing
Patrizia Forlin

Editorial coordination
Sara Albano
Armando Albanesi

Cover concept
Colin Carruthers

Graphics
Marco Cordiani

Printing
P.R.A.V. Studio Srl
Str Eugeniu De Savoya, 11
Timisoara (Romania)
pravstudiosrl@yahoo.com

Cover photo
Stefano Mileto
www.stefanomileto.com

Photo of recipes
Autentica Srl and Circolo dei Buongustai archive

ISBN 978-88-906784-3-1

Many thanks to: Virginia Giusti, Maria Giulia Santini

La mia Cucina 100 RECIPES

introducing

FABIO CAMPOLI

Italy's favourite celebrity chef

VIVE PER MANGIARE

TONY MACAR⬤NI

Autentica Edizioni

MEETING FABIO CAMPOLI

Fabio, after almost thirty years since you started out on your career, today you are a versatile chef of international renown: experimenter, television personality, consultant and gastronomy lecturer, spokesperson for products, author of books, an expert on food design, and so on and so forth. But what is the driving force behind this great passion for cooking?

What drives the passion of a chef, as well as any other gourmet, are the various food resources, which over the centuries have increasingly made cooking an almost inexhaustible source of history, ideas, combinations, which almost like magic come alive in different ways in every part of the world.

It is precisely through knowledge and continuous study that culinary horizons expand, allowing me to perform every task with which I am entrusted with a sense of inquisitiveness and passion.

So, it seems that even though you have been dealing with food on a daily basis for almost thirty years, you still have some hidden gastronomic desires ...

Absolutely, and I want to emphasize that for me "gastronomic desire" follows two connected but separate paths, namely that of research and innovation that merges with that of history and tradition. I love to bring ancient dishes back to life, and I am always looking for new ways to excite people through a dish and its history.

Gastronomic desires aside - but which I want to mention because they unite each one of us - there are those desires related to the nostalgia of a dish, the flavour of which is alive within us because it is linked to people, places, and adventures that have made a deep impression on our lives. It is exactly in this evocation of the hidden desires within my dinner guests that I find the inspiration to revive emotions in the kitchen that in reality never truly left.

Is there a time of day that you consider the most fruitful for formulating your dishes, since you are always very busy during the day?

Usually I can give the best of myself from five in the afternoon until late at night. And once I get going, I could go on indefinitely. This is because the various activities for which I was lucky enough to have been chosen to do by many Italian companies and entrepreneurs, led me to become an even more anomalous chef, because I became a sort of happy wanderer. My personal upsurge of creative energy finds its peak in the silence of my home in the country, when, in peaceful solitude, ideas that were conceived during the day float to the surface, become firmly rooted in the mind and duly meditated upon. Recipes, stories, people, new flavours, products tasted, wake up as if by magic, always shaping themselves into something new.

There is often, then, a kind of "dream dimension" prior to the preparation of your recipes?

To be honest it is exactly like that, because to develop a recipe I proceed as if I were in a dream, closing my eyes and, with the help of my brain's archive of flavours, it is as if were actually tasting the combinations that I have in mind to create. It's like saying I eat what I cook "in my imagination", before it becomes reality. It's a legacy that comes from many years spent in television devising recipes one after the other, often not having the time needed to try them out: in some cases I even had to cook a dish for the very first time in the studio, when on air!

It seems that for you preparing a dish is comparable to the writing a musical piece...

In a certain sense it is like this, because a recipe is like a melody, it has its own tones, its own "high" and "low" qualities. And every chef interprets the ingredients in their own way, according to the score that suits them most, as well as dictated by basic experience. The comparison with music is really quite apt because I am passionate about music, and I myself play the piano and I love to do so whenever I can. It is nice to hear the sound of the notes, but it is also just as pleasant to taste those of the ingredients, trying to put them together in the most harmonious way possible.

Is wellness a constant in your recipes?

It is one of the aspects that I pay the most attention to, because I firmly believe that the combination of healthy and tasty food is possible. The paths that not only a chef but each one of us can follow to reach it are often inherent in small everyday actions, such as choosing to eat more fruits and vegetables, eating food following the rule of "cheap but good", varying one's foods avoiding junk food as far as possible, and rediscovering the pleasure (thanks also to the help of modern appliances) of home cooking.

Food affects our health in terms of mood, weight, disease prevention, and the correct intake of essential micronutrients. I'm glad that healthy cooking is a growing phenomenon, but it is up to each one of us to pursue this goal.

Do you think that cooking is an art?

I see a chef as being closer to a craftsman, equipped with manual skills, creativity and inspiration, often able to realize creations of extraordinary flavour. What distinguishes cooking from art is that the latter is durable over time, a dish on the other hand is a snapshot of the moment, a "temporary" creation, as well as hedonistic by nature.

While not owning your own restaurant, you are called to deal with the analysis of the customers of many businesses in the industry. How would you define your approach to the customer?

To understand the needs of those on the other side, i.e. at the table, the secret is simply to put yourself in their shoes. I think that often there is no bigger mistake than to base your business decisions on completely personal tastes. My relationship with the client is also affected by my experience as a regular customer, who when going to a restaurant expects not only to eat well, but also to feel comfortable and be treated with respect and consideration by the staff, according to the basic rules of hospitality.

Are you jealous of your professional secrets?

I decided to base my professional career on sharing in 2006, when I founded the Circolo dei Buongustai (Circle of Gourmets) together with my partners. It is through this association that I started to extend my favourite activities even

further, such as teaching, "making culture" through food, and passing on what I have learned in years of varied experiences. I could never be jealous of my culinary knowledge. But it is also true that we must be careful not to waste energy and knowledge acquired in the field with people who are not truly able to make use of it. For this reason, from all my co-workers I always demand attention, commitment and dedication.

How has your cooking changed over the years?

As happens to most people, especially in cooking, I also had to do my apprenticeship for some years, which tied me to other people's cooking techniques and the culinary trends of the moment. Later I chose to free myself of every culinary dogma, oral or written, entrusting my daily work to experience, emotions and feelings, the primary ingredients of all my recipes. From then on, everything good that has happened to me came spontaneously.

How do you see the future of catering?

I think there are still a lot of untapped potential and new paths to explore. But what I consider even more important nowadays is that the concept of professional ethics needs to be respected, something that is essential in any workplace, and which is linked to many aspects, involving the relationship with employees and with customers. Those who choose to work in catering should never forget that they have chosen a job in the service of others, and even if only for this reason, it is something that is truly ennobling.

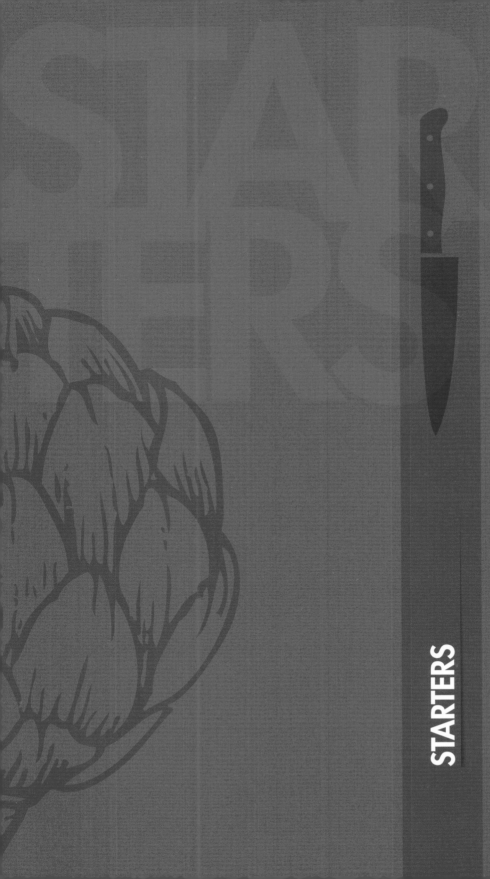

STARTERS

RICE AND PECORINO CROQUETTES STUFFED WITH MUSSELS AND CHERRY TOMATOES

SERVES **4**

250 g basic risotto*
150 g grated Pecorino cheese
Black pepper to taste
1 l vegetable stock*
400 g mussels
1 clove garlic
15 g '00' flour

5 tbsp extra virgin olive oil
100 g cherry tomatoes
4 sprigs parsley
Flour and water batter*
300 g grated potatoes
Oil for frying, as needed

METHOD

Prepare a basic risotto with vegetable stock, remove from the heat and add the oil, Pecorino and pepper.
Place on a large tray and leave to cool.
Put two tablespoons of olive oil and the garlic into a frying pan.
Heat, add the mussels and cover.
Turn off the heat as soon as the mussels open, shell the mussels and cut them into small pieces.
Put two tablespoons of olive oil into a frying pan and add the mussel liquor, the cherry tomatoes cut into four pieces, the mussels and chopped parsley. Cook for a few minutes.
Separately, in a bowl, mix one tablespoon of flour and one of oil to be used for thickening the sauce.
Add the thickener to the tomatoes and cook until the mixture thickens.
When cold, it will be a soft and substantial filling.
Form rolls with the filling and place inside the rice; then form them into croquettes. Dip the croquettes in the batter and roll them in grated potato.
Wrap them in plastic wrap as if making a sweet and let them sit in the fridge.
Deep fry in oil shortly before serving.

MINI BREAD BALLS PIE
WITH SALAMI AND VEGETABLES

SERVES **10**

400 g pizza dough*
300 g celery
300 g onion
300 g carrots
500 g salami

10 g dill
300 g tomato passata
2 g dried oregano
5 tbsp extra virgin olive oil
Fine salt to taste

METHOD

Peel, wash and cut the vegetables into small cubes.

Dice the salami.

Arrange the vegetables on a baking sheet, season with salt, olive oil and chopped dill.

Bake in the oven at 140° C for 20 minutes.

Once cooked, leave to cool.

Now, take the pizza dough and form mini bread balls.

Put a cube of salami and some cooked vegetables in the centre of each one; close the dough around them to form a ball (cutting).

Arrange the mini balls thus obtained in a 28 cm baking to allow for uniform cooking.

It is important to oil the dish well because oil is an excellent conductor of heat and allows a crust to form.

Put the tomato passata into a bowl, season with salt, oregano and 2 tablespoons of olive oil.

Put a teaspoon of tomato sauce on each roll and leave to rise for another 30 minutes.

Bake at 180° C for 35 minutes.

CHICKPEA FLOUR AND ROSEMARY FARINATA WITH MORTADELLA

SERVES **4**

500 g chickpea flour
1.5 l water
100 ml extra virgin olive oil
3 sprigs rosemary

1 clove garlic
8 thin slices mortadella
100 g Grana Padano cheese
Fine salt to taste

METHOD

Prepare the flavoured oil by putting the oil, garlic and rosemary sprigs into a saucepan.
Cover and cook for 15 minutes on a low heat.
In a bowl, work the chickpea flour with warm water and salt and leave to stand for 5 hours.
Line a round mould with baking paper and oil the bottom with the flavoured oil.
Pour in the chickpea flour mixture and bake at 250° C for 15 minutes.
Serve the farinata hot with the slices of mortadella and shavings of Grana Padano cheese.

BLACK OLIVES CRACKERS WITH HAM

SERVES **4**

1 **kg** white flour
20 **g** sugar
440 **g** water
25 **g** dry yeast
80 **g** Taggiasche olives
160 **g** extra virgin olive oil

15 **g** salt
2 mozzarella cheeses
2 slices ham
White wine vinegar to taste
2 tomatoes

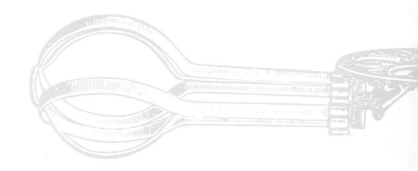

METHOD

Put the dry yeast into a bowl with the sugar and water, dissolve well.
Add the flour and, after working the dough a little, add the salt, olive oil and chopped olives, continue to knead.
Leave to rise for at least 10 hours in the refrigerator in a container covered with lightly perforated plastic wrap.
Roll out the dough by hand, form into disks the size of a biscuit.
Place the disks on a lightly oiled baking sheet and bake at 170° C for 10 minutes.
Once cooked, cut the biscuits in half and return to the oven at 140° C to dry them out.
Once cool, before serving, dip the biscuits quickly in water and vinegar, and fill them with sliced tomato, sliced mozzarella and ham.

OLIVE RISSOLES

SERVES 4

200 g stewing beef
2 tbsp extra virgin olive oil
2 cloves garlic
2 sprigs rosemary
100 g mortadella
200 g very thick béchamel*

2 egg yolks
2 g nutmeg
Fine salt to taste
Bread crumbs, to taste
2 beaten eggs
Oil for frying, as needed

METHOD

Place the oil and garlic in a saucepan and heat. Add the meat, rosemary and salt. Sauté then deglaze with the white wine and cook off the alcohol. Cook with the lid on for an hour.
Once the meat is cooked, add the diced mortadella and then the thick béchamel sauce.
Turn off, add the egg yolks and nutmeg and mix well.
Pass through a meat grinder.
Leave to rest in the fridge for an hour before rolling into balls the size of an "olive".
Dip the balls first into the egg and then into the bread crumbs, repeat this operation twice.
Deep fry in hot oil, a few at a time, and drain on a paper towel.

RUSTIC ARTICHOKE PUFF

SERVES **4**

400 g puff pastry
200 g very thick béchamel*
100 g artichoke cream
3 eggs

2 sprigs parsley
Fine salt to taste
Black pepper to taste
Egg for brushing

METHOD

Mix the béchamel with the artichoke cream, egg yolks and chopped parsley.
Beat the egg whites separately, stir a little of the egg white into the béchamel and
artichoke mixture to make it looser then add the rest stirring gently with a whisk.
This will allow the mixture to rise better in the oven.
Roll out the puff pastry with a rolling pin to a thickness of half a centimetre,
place a plate on the pastry and cut around it to get a disc then prick it lightly all
over with a fork.
Put a sheet of parchment on a baking sheet and place the puff pastry disc on top.
Put the béchamel and artichoke mix on the puff pastry disc and close it by
bringing the sides to the centre creating a square and then bringing the corners
of the square to the centre.
Brush with beaten egg.
Bake at 170 ° for 30 minutes.

DUMPLINGS ON SALSA VERDE

SERVES **4**

250 **g** pizza dough*
300 **g** boiled meat*
200 **g** cooked chard
FOR THE SALSA VERDE
80 **g** parsley
4 fillets anchovies
1 clove garlic

6 capers
2 hard boiled egg yolks
50 **g** vinegar
100 **g** extra virgin olive oil
60 **g** stale bread
Black pepper to taste
Fine salt to taste

METHOD

Cut the boiled meat and chard into large pieces and add them to the pizza dough.
Mix quickly in a kitchen machine.
Leave to rise for another thirty minutes.
Roll the dough into balls.
Put the water, vinegar and salt into a saucepan on the heat.
When the water simmers, immerse the balls of dough in it a few at a time.
When they float, wait for one minute, remove and drain on a cloth.
Leave them to dry.
Arrange the balls on a lightly oiled baking sheet and bake in a preheated oven
at 180° C until golden brown.
Serve the balls accompanied by a small bowl of salsa verde.

FOR THE SALSA VERDE

Place the parsley, capers, egg yolks, garlic, bread, anchovies, vinegar, salt and
pepper into a mixer and, while the mixer is running, add the oil in a thin stream
to obtain a soft textured sauce.

PASTRY ROLLS WITH ARTICHOKES AND EGGS

SERVES **4**

100 **g** filo pastry
30 **g** melted butter
2 artichokes
1 shallot
2 sprigs fennel fronds
2 lemons

2 **tbsp** extra virgin olive oil
150 **g** sliced ham
4 eggs
Fine salt to taste
100 **g** fresh salad

METHOD

Prepare the artichokes by removing the tough outer leaves until you get to
the most tender part, remove the tough part of the stem and the outer fibrous
layer. Halve the artichokes, remove the hair inside and put them in a bowl with
cold water and the juice of one lemon.
Cut the artichokes into very thin strips (julienne), chop the shallots and fennel
fronds and toss in a bowl with salt and two tablespoons of oil.
Cook in a frying pan without stirring.
Beat the eggs with the salt, a dash of lemon juice and the grated lemon zest.
Scramble the eggs in a frying pan with a tablespoon of oil.
Season with salt and pour over seared artichokes.
Separately, open the filo pastry, brush one sheet with melted butter then cover
with another sheet.
Cut into strips (4). Put the ham and egg and artichokes and egg mixture on top.
Roll up into a bundle and place the closed side downwards. They should be long
narrow rolls (like cannelloni). Bake in preheated oven at 160° C for 15-20 minutes.
Cut the rolls into oblique slices. Serve on a bed of salad.

RUSTIC PIE WITH RICE AND RED ONIONS

SERVES 6

150 g sliced ham
100 g blanched cabbage leaves
200 g boiled rice
3 whole eggs
125 ml milk
150 g red onions

1 bay leaf
2 tbsp white wine vinegar
2 sage leaves
50 g grated Parmesan cheese
2 tbsp extra virgin olive oil
Fine salt to taste

METHOD

Cut the onion into thin strips (julienne) and cook in a saucepan with the oil, vinegar, shredded sage and bay leave.
Cook over low heat and add a little water if required.
When cooked, season it with a little salt and remove the bay leaf.
Beat the eggs with a pinch of salt and the milk in a bowl.
Add the cold boiled rice and onions to the mixture.
Use a rolling pin to flatten and soften the cabbage leaves.
Line the tin with the cabbage leaves and cover the bottom with the ham.
Pour in the rice mixture and cover with another layer of cabbage leaves, tucking the edges in well and cover with grated Parmesan cheese.
Bake in a preheated oven at 200° C for at least 25 minutes.

PORK SAUSAGE ROLL
WITH BROCCOLI AND SHRIMPS

SERVES 4

4 sheets filo pastry
40 g butter
200 g broccoli
200 g pork sausage
½ glass white wine
8 shrimps
3 g marjoram

FOR THE SALAD
2 tomatoes
1 sprig parsley
Fine salt to taste
Juice of 1 lemon
1 tbsp extra virgin olive oil

METHOD

Wash the tomatoes, cut into cubes and place in a bowl.
Add the chopped parsley and season with salt, lemon juice and olive oil. Keep to one side.
Cut the cooked sausage into small cubes, put them in a saucepan with the white wine, let it boil, if you wish, you can remove the fat from the surface as boils using a slotted spoon.
Cook until it the liquid has evaporated then remove from heat, leave to cool and chop everything. Keep to one side.
Meanwhile, boil the broccoli, drain and sauté in a frying pan with the olive oil.
Shell the shrimp, cut into small pieces, place in a bowl and toss with a little salt and marjoram. Keep them aside.
On a flat surface, layer the sheets of filo pastry one on top of the other, brushing each sheet with melted butter before placing another on top. Make four layers.
In the centre of each put the broccoli, cover with shrimps and place a small amount of chopped sausage on top.
Roll everything up, taking care to place the closure at the bottom.
Bake in the oven at 160° C for at least ten minutes.
Remove the roll from the oven, leave to stand for five minutes, slice with a serrated knife and serve each portion accompanied by a spoonful of tomato salad.

HONEY AND CHICKPEA FRITTERS

SERVES **8**

250 g chickpea flour
250 g water
25 g honey
25 g chopped parsley

40 g breadcrumbs
1 bunch rosemary, tied
5 ml extra virgin olive oil
Salt to taste

METHOD

Put the water, rosemary, garlic, salt and honey into a saucepan and simmer for 5 minutes.

Turn off the heat and leave to infuse for 10 minutes.

Use a whisk to mix in the chickpea flour as you add it gradually (making sure that the water is warm but not hot, otherwise lumps will easily form).

Return to the heat, stirring occasionally with a whisk until the flour thickens.

At this point, cover with the lid, reduce the heat to low and simmer for about 40 minutes.

At the end, remove from heat and add the chopped parsley and bread.

In the meantime, get an empty 500 ml plastic bottle. Make small holes in the bottom and cleanly cut off the top with scissors, so you have a hollow cylinder.

Pour the mixture into the dampened bottle, press it down and leave in the refrigerator for at least 10 hours.

When the mixture is solid, remove from the mould, first cut in half lengthwise then cut many crescents about 1.5 cm thick.

Deep fry them, drain and serve, accompanied by lemon wedges to squeeze over at the moment of eating.

COD PEARLS

SERVES **4**

250 g cod fillet
100 g white bread, crusts removed
2 sprigs parsley
1 whole egg
Salt to taste
250 ml milk
90 g flour

100 g butter
1 tbsp extra virgin olive oil
Juice and zest of ½ lemon

FOR THE BREADING
3 whole eggs
Bread crumbs as required

METHOD

Make a light roux in a saucepan by cooking the melted butter and the flour added gradually for about 7-8 minutes.

Then add the milk to the roux, bring to the boil and cook until you get a thick bechamel. Leave to cool.

Separately, cut the cod fillet into cubes and put it in a frying pan with the oil, cover and cook it on a low heat.

Add the fish cubes to the pan with the bechamel and cook for another few minutes. Remove from heat and add the peeled and chopped white bread, whole egg, parsley, salt and the lemon juice and zest.

Blend the mixture with a stick blender. Leave to cool in the refrigerator until it solidifies.

Shape the mixture into "pearls," small balls weighing about 10 g and put them in the refrigerator to cool.

Then, coat the pearls in beaten egg and bread crumbs. Put them back in the refrigerator to cool.

Fry in plenty of oil for about 2 minutes and serve hot accompanied by lemon wedges.

SARDINES IN ONION BATTER WITH SWEET AND SOUR, PINE NUTS AND RAISINS

SERVES **4**

20 fresh sardines
50 g "00" flour
Peanut oil for frying
FOR THE BATTER
100 g "00" flour
100 g corn starch

20 g raisins
50 g pine nuts
4 sprigs chervil
170 g cold sparkling water
50 g red onion
4 tbsp vinegar
1 tbsp sugar

METHOD

Slice the onions thinly and place in a saucepan with vinegar, salt and sugar.
Cover and cook on a low heat until the liquid evaporates and the onions are dry.
Wash the raisins and rehydrate them in water, drain, squeeze and chop together
with the pine nuts.
Combine the flour, corn starch, raisins, pine nuts, dried chervil and onion in a bowl.
Mix the ingredients and add the water. Mix the mixture well. It must be quite
thick: the batter must stick to the surface of the spoon when you hold it up.
Cover with plastic wrap and leave to rest in the refrigerator for 30 minutes.
Clean the sardines and place in refrigerator (they must be well cold, almost frozen).
When you are ready to use them, roll them in flour and then put them
immediately in a sieve.
Leave sardines to rest for 5 minutes, then dip them in batter and deep fry in hot oil.
Drain the sardines on paper towels.
Prepare a mixed salad, toss in a bowl with the salt, vinegar and olive oil and
serve it as an accompaniment to the sardines in batter.

POTATOES AND BEETROOT TURBANS WITH A CENTRE OF GOOSE SALAMI

SERVES **4**

500 **g** potatoes
100 **g** butter
2 eggs
200 **g** boiled beetroot

200 **g** boiled green beans
200 **g** goose salami
Linseeds to taste
Fine salt to taste

METHOD

Boil the potatoes in their skins in a saucepan with a generous amount of salt. When cooked, mash quickly. Place them in a saucepan, add salt, melted butter and eggs and mix well.

Keep part of the mashed potatoes the natural colour and colour the other part with boiled, chopped beetroot.

Put the two mixtures in two piping bags.

Grease a baking tray and make baskets with the light puree, in the middle of which you are going to put the chopped green beans and the goose salami.

Close the basket using the red puree.

Sprinkle with linseed and bake at 200° C.

Leave to rest before serving.

AUBEGINE BALLS WITH SMOKED PROVOLA CHEESE

SERVES **5/6**

400 g aubergine
60 g breadcrumbs
60 g Parmigiano-Reggiano (Parmesan)
120 g smoked provola cheese, cubed
Black pepper to taste

1 handful chopped parsley
2 eggs
2 cloves garlic
Salt to taste
½ **tsp** chilli (preferably in cream)

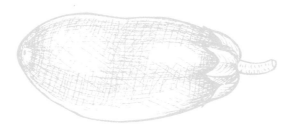

METHOD

Wash and dry the aubergine.
Make 2-3 incisions in the outer skin and spike them with slivers of garlic.
Place them on an oven shelf and cook in a preheated oven at 200° C. They are
cooked when the skin tends to peel off easily from the pulp and the pulp is soft
to the touch.
At this point, remove from the oven and place them in a bowl then seal hermetically
plastic wrap to allow the steam to further facilitate the removal of the skin.
When cool, peel the aubergine and put the pulp into a colander to drain the
excess water, press them a little to facilitate the operation.
Put the pulp into a bowl and add the eggs, breadcrumbs, grated cheese, crushed
garlic, salt, pepper, chilli and parsley.
Stir to mix the ingredients well and then shape into round balls the size of a
walnut (you should get about 30), which you stuff with a cube of provola cheese.
Dip the balls in the beaten egg and then in bread crumbs.
Deep fry in plenty of oil and serve hot.

SUPER SANDWICHES

SANDWICH WITH FRITTATA, ASPARAGUS, TOMATO AND CHEESE

SERVES **4**

350 g bread
400 g asparagus
4 frittatas*
100 g tomato sauce*
200 g Caciocavallo cheese

4 pieces dried tomato
2 g oregano
2 leaves basil
Fine salt to taste
Extra virgin olive oil to taste

METHOD

Wash asparagus. Peel them with a vegetable peeler, removing the lower part of the stem that is tough.

Tie the asparagus in a bunch with string and cook them "standing" in a basket with the tips out of the water boiling. Once cooked remove them from the water and leave to cool.

Take the stale bread, like ciabatta, cut it open and sprinkle with the tomato sauce, the chopped, dried tomatoes, oregano and basil.

Prepare the frittatas and, once cold, use them to wrap the asparagus.

Put the rolled frittatas in the sandwich and finish the filling with the cheese cut into thin strips.

Put the top on the sandwich and wrap it in aluminium.

Bake at 220° C for about 5 minutes.

Remove the aluminium and cut the bread into slices, serve with a dash of olive oil.

SWEET&SALTY SANDWICH

SERVES **4**

600 g pizza dough*
400 g roast pork*
1 sprig rosemary
100 g onions in sweet and sour sauce*

3 tbsp extra virgin olive oil
200 g white grapes
150 g salad mix

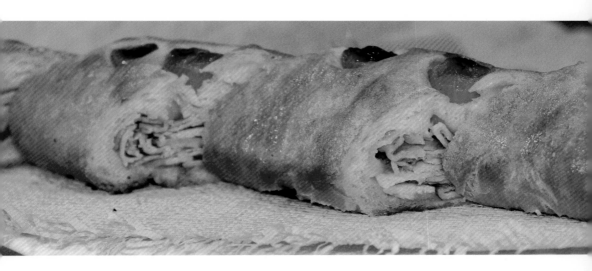

METHOD

Thinly sliced roast pork and season with chopped rosemary, onions and olive oil.
Roll out the pizza dough to a thickness of 1 cm and cut into rectangles that are
going to be filled with the seasoned pork.
Join the long sides of the rectangle together and pinch with your fingers to seal.
Then, place the roll on a greased baking tray with the join side down.
Use scissors to make cuts along the entire length and arrange the grapes in them.
Bake in a preheated oven at 170° C for 30 minutes.
Serve the sandwich with fresh salad.

WHAT A GOOD SANDWICH!

SERVES **4**

400 **g** sirloin steak
1 **tbsp** mustard
150 **g** rocket
200 **g** cherry tomatoes
1 **tbsp** chopped red onion
Fine salt to taste
1 **tbsp** extra virgin olive oil

FOR THE FLATBREAD
500 **g** flour
100 **g** lard
100 **ml** water
Fine salt to taste
2 **tbsp** sesame seeds

METHOD

For the flatbread

Mix the flour with lard, water and salt until you get elastic dough.
Leave to rest covered with foil.
Roll out the dough, sprinkle with sesame seeds and press well with a rolling pin
so that they stick to the flatbread. Use a plate to cut out of discs.
Cook the flatbreads on both sides in a lightly oiled frying pan.
Put the flatbreads into a plastic bag while still hot; this will keep them soft and
ready to be rolled up.

For the meat

Remove the connective tissue from the meat and give it a uniform shape.
Salt and oil the meat on both sides.
Bake on the griddle for 3 minutes per side.
Leave it to rest at the edge of the griddle for 3 minutes.
Meanwhile, place the rocket in a bowl, with the cherry tomatoes cut into
quarters and season with salt and oil.
Spread the mustard on the flatbread then arrange the chopped onion and
rocket salad and cherry tomatoes on top.
Finish by stuffing the flatbread with the strips of meat.
Roll up the flatbread and enjoy.

AUTUMN SANDWICH

SERVES **4**

1/2 brioche bread
1 game salami sausage
200 g pumpkin
150 g fresh salted cheese
2 tbsp honey

2 sprigs celery leaves
1 cup low-fat yoghurt
Juice of 1 lemon
50 g onion
Fine salt to taste

METHOD

Grill the pumpkin on the griddle for 2 minutes per side.
Put the celery leaves in a bowl and season with lemon juice, a pinch of salt, onion and finally the yoghurt, blend with a stick blender and get the sauce for the sandwich.
Slice the salami, the fresh cheese and the brioche and set aside.
Proceed as follows:
Put a slice of bread as the base, sprinkle with a thin layer of sauce, pumpkin, another slice of bread, salami, even more bread, honey, cheese, bread, more of the sauce, pumpkin, bread, salami, bread, honey, cheese and finally bread.
Skewer the stuffed half brioche with toothpicks, so it will be easier to cut it into 6 parts and serve.

PASTA

SPAGHETTI WITH MARINATED ANCHOVIES AND FENNEL WITH BREAD CRUMBS AND OLIVES

SERVES **4**

300 g spaghetti
2 fennel bulbs
400 g cleaned anchovies
2 tbsp white wine vinegar

Fine salt to taste
5 tbsp extra virgin olive oil
150 g sandwich bread
100 g green olives

METHOD

Put the anchovies in a pan and season with salt, vinegar and oil.
Store them in a refrigerator for two hours.
Cook the pasta in plenty of boiling salted water.
Wash, peel and thinly slice the fennel.
Add it to the pasta towards the end of cooking.
Meanwhile, chop the olives with the bread crumbs and toast them in a pan.
When the pasta is almost cooked, fry the anchovies in a frying pan over a medium heat
Drain the pasta with fennel and pour into the frying pan with the anchovies, toss quickly.
Serve the pasta sprinkled with the toasted bread with olives and a dribble of olive oil.

PACCHERI WITH TOMATO, BASIL AND MOZZARELLA

SERVES **4**

300 g paccheri
60 g white onion
5 tbsp extra virgin olive oil
450 g peeled tomatoes
12 leaves basil

300 g mozzarella
1 lemon
40 g Parmesan cheese
Fine salt to taste

METHOD

Chop the mozzarella and place in a bowl. Toss with lemon juice and set aside.
Cook the pasta in plenty of boiling salted water.
Chop the onion and place in a saucepan with the oil.
Cook on low heat.
Put the peeled tomato and the previously cooked and salted onion into a saucepan.
When the sauce starts to thicken, add the basil.
Drain the pasta, add it to the tomato sauce, stir and turn off.
Off the heat, add the mozzarella and mix well.
Serve the pasta with a sprinkling of grated Parmesan cheese.

PAPPARDELLE WITH CUTTLEFISH, LEEK MILK AND PESTO

SERVES **4**

350 g pappardelle
2 cuttlefish
3 sprigs thyme
2 leeks
1 cup milk

20 g butter
120 g Ligurian pesto
1 lemon
Fine salt to taste
Extra virgin olive oil to taste

METHOD

Wash and clean the leeks.
Chop finely and place in a saucepan with the butter and milk.
Cover and cook on low heat for at least thirty minutes.
Add salt and blend the leeks with a stick blender.
Clean the squid and cut into thin strips.
Put the cuttlefish in a bowl and season with thyme, salt and two tablespoons of olive oil.
Cook the pasta in plenty of boiling salted water.
Separately, heat a frying pan and sear the cuttlefish.
Drain the pasta and toss with the creamed leeks and pesto.
Serve in a flat-bottomed bowl by pouring the pasta over the cooked cuttlefish.
Finish with some grated lemon zest.

BALSAMIC PASTA WITH BRUNOISE OF VEGETABLES AND MORTADELLA

SERVES **4**

250 g trofie
1 onion
100 g button muchrooms
100 g peppers
100 g courgettes
200 g mortadella
2 sprigs thyme
60 g sifted bread crumbs
2 tbsp extra virgin olive oil
Fine salt to taste

FOR THE VINAIGRETTE
30 g balsamic vinegar
Fine salt to taste
100 g extra virgin olive oil

METHOD

Cook the pasta in plenty of boiling salted water.
Wash and clean the vegetables.
Cut the onion, mushrooms, courgettes and peppers into 2 mm cubes.
Put the oil in a frying pan, add the vegetables, season with salt and cook with the lid on.
Cut the mortadella into small cubes, the same size as the vegetables.
Towards the end of cooking add the mortadella, thyme and bread.
Prepare the vinaigrette in a small bowl by dissolving the salt in the vinegar and emulsifying with a stream of oil.
Drain the pasta, season it first with the vinaigrette and then with the rest of the seasoning.
Serve the pasta in a bowl.

SPAGHETTI WITH SQUID, PINE NUTS, HARD-BOILED EGG YOLK AND GOMASIO

SERVES **4**

280 **g** spaghetti
300 **g** fresh squid
10 **g** ginger
5 **tbsp** extra virgin olive oil
1 **tbsp** gomasio
10 sheets seaweed

20 **g** pine nuts
4 hard-boiled egg yolks
2 sprigs parsley
Fine salt to taste
Black pepper to taste

METHOD

Cook the pasta in plenty of boiling salted water.
Clean the squid, dry them well and cut them into thin strips.
Mix the calamari, gomasio, ginger and chopped seaweed in a bowl.
Mix and sear in a hot frying pan without oil for a few minutes.
In the meantime, toast the pine nuts and sieve the yolks.
Drain the pasta into the pan of calamari and saute with a little of the cooking water.
Serve the pasta in a hot dish sprinkled with pine nuts, sieved egg yolks, chopped parsley and a drizzle of olive oil.

GNOCCHI WITH MUSHROOMS, GORGONZOLA, SPINACH AND POMEGRANATE

SERVES **4**

1 **kg** gnocchi flavoured with mushrooms*
200 **ml** fresh Cream
200 **g** gorgonzola
½ cup grappa

100 **g** spinach
50 **g** pomegranate
Fine salt to taste
50 **g** grated Parmesan cheese

METHOD

Cut the gorgonzola into cubes.
Put the cream in a saucepan, let it warm slightly and add the gorgonzola and grappa. Melt everything over a low heat.
Wash the spinach and remove the stems.
Chop and add to the sauce off the heat.
Put the sauce back on the stove on a low heat.
Cook the gnocchi in boiling salted water, count one minute after they float to the top then switch off.
Drain well and add to the sauce. Mix well.
Add the Parmesan and stir well.
Put the mushroom gnocchi in a bowl and sprinkle with raw spinach and pomegranate seeds.

GNOCCHI WITH SAUSAGE, ROCKET SAUCE AND CRISPY BREAD CRUMBS

SERVES 4

400 g potato gnocchi
2 sausages
½ cup white wine
200 g rocket
100 g sliced bread
2 sprigs parsley

1 clove garlic
Fine salt to taste
Coarse Fine salt to taste
5 tbsp extra virgin olive oil
120 g salted ricotta

METHOD

Remove the skin from the sausage and break into small pieces with your hands and place in a saucepan with the white wine and a tablespoon of olive oil.
Cook over a low heat until the fat has melted and the sausage is cooked.
Coarsely mix the sliced bread in a blender with parsley and garlic then gradually pour in three tablespoons of oil.
Cook the bread in a frying pan for a few minutes until crispy.
Fill a pan with water and boil.
Add the coarse salt, when it is dissolved, cook the gnocchi a few at a time.
When they rise to the surface, count one minute then drain and add to the pan with the sausage.

For the rocket sauce
Boil the rocket for one minute in the gnocchi cooking water, blend, adding half a cup of water and two tablespoons of olive oil.
Put two tablespoons of rocket sauce in the bottom of a dish, put the gnocchi on top and sprinkle with grated ricotta.

HONEY TAGLIOLINI
WITH CREAM AND PUMPKIN

SERVES **4**

500 g egg pasta with honey*
350 g pumpkin
80 g leeks
60 g carrots
2 bay leaves

200 ml water
1 cup cream
12 toasted pumpkin seeds
60 g grated Parmesan cheese
2 tbsp extra virgin olive oil

METHOD

Wash and peel the pumpkin and carrots.
Peel and wash the leeks.
Cut the pumpkin, carrots and leeks into large pieces.
Place the oil, vegetables, 100 ml water and bay leaf into a saucepan, cover and cook on a low heat. Add salt to season.
Once the vegetables are cooked, remove the bay leaves, blend everything and keep warm.
Put the cream in a saucepan with 100 ml of water and heat.
Cook the tagliolini in boiling salted water.
Drain the pasta and put them in the cream. Mix.
Turn off, add the grated cheese and then mix well.
Put a spoonful of pumpkin cream in the bottom of a dish, put the tagliolini on top and sprinkle with toasted pumpkin seeds.

POTATO AND HAM RAVIOLI WITH LEMON OIL AND HAZELNUTS

SERVES **4**

FOR THE FRESH EGG PASTA
125 g "00" flour
125 g semolina flour
1 egg
175 g water
2 g salt

FOR THE FILLING
300 g potatoes
150 g ham
100 g mascarpone
Nutmeg, cinnamon and black pepper to taste

FOR THE DRESSING
4 tbsp extra virgin olive oil
1 lemon
60 g roasted hazelnuts
100 g caciocavallo cheese

METHOD

For the fresh pasta: Put the flour, semolina, egg, salt and water into the kitchen machine. Mix with the hook until it forms smooth, uniform and homogeneous dough. Leave the dough to rest in the refrigerator for at least 2 hours covered with plastic wrap.

For the filling: Put the potatoes into a saucepan with cold, salted water, cover, bring to the boil and cook.

Once cooked, peel and mash the potatoes while they are still hot. Leave them to cool.

Chop the ham with a knife and add it to the cold boiled potatoes.

Season the filling with a pinch of nutmeg, cinnamon and pepper and finally add the mascarpone. Mix well and put the mixture in the refrigerator.

For the dressing: Put the oil, the lemon zest and juice into a frying pan. Do not heat too much otherwise the lemon juice may be spoiled. Separately, toast the hazelnuts in a small pan. Keep to one side.

To complete the dish: Roll out the dough thinly. Fill a piping bag with the filling and pipe onto the strips of dough, fold them over cut into square ravioli with a wheel cutter.

Boil the ravioli in salted water.

Assemble the dish by placing 4 ravioli per portion in the bottom of the dish, pour on the lemon sauce, sprinkle with nuts and garnish with grated cheese.

EGG PASTA ROLL WITH BACON, SPINACH AND RICOTTA

SERVES **4**

300 g egg pasta *
300 g ricotta
200 g spinach
8 slices bacon
60 g butter

80 g grated cheese
1 tbsp poppy seeds
White pepper to taste
Fine salt to taste

METHOD

Wash and clean the spinach.
Boil the spinach in salted boiling water for 5 minutes. Drain well.
Put the ricotta, a pinch of white pepper, chopped spinach and salt into a bowl. Mix well.
Melt the butter with the poppy seeds in a frying pan; this will be the dressing for our roll.
Roll out the pasta quite thick and place on a cloth.
Arrange the slices of bacon on the whole length of the pasta.
Spread the spinach and ricotta mixture evenly over the bacon.
Roll up the pasta lengthwise with the aid of the cloth and fasten it with a string for roasts.
Bake the pasta roll in a fish-kettle with boiling salted water for 15 minutes.
Leave it to rest for 15 minutes.
Remove the cloth and cut the roll into slices about 2 cm thick.
Serve the slices with the melted butter flavoured with poppy seeds and grated cheese.

TORTELLONI WITH SQUACQUERONE CHEESE IN EGG AND WHITE ASPARAGUS SAUCE

SERVES **4**

300 g egg pasta*
200 g Squacquerone cheese
4 hard-boiled egg yolks
1 tsp saffron
1 shot Gentian liqueur

60 g butter
3 sage leaves
400 g white asparagus
100 g Piave cheese

METHOD

Wash asparagus. Peel them with a vegetable peeler, removing the lower part of the stem that is tough.
Cut the asparagus obliquely.
Melt the butter with the sage in a frying pan, add the asparagus and a pinch of salt, cover and cook on a gentle heat.
Prepare the filling for the tortelli:
Blend the egg yolks, saffron and gentian with a stick blender, season with salt.
Roll out the dough thinly and cut into squares, in the centre of each put the stuffing you have just blended and a teaspoon of squacquerone cheese.
Use a brush to brush the edges of the pasta with beaten egg.
Fold in half giving the classic shape of tortello.
Boil the tortelli in a large quantity of salted water.
Drain and put in the frying pan with the butter and asparagus and sauté.
Serve the tortelloni in a hot dish and sprinkle with the grated cheese.

PASTA AND BEAN PIE

SERVES 4

250 g mezze maniche pasta
300 g boiled borlotti beans
350 g celery, carrots and onions
100 g white bread crumbs
100 g grated Parmesan cheese

4 tbsp extra virgin olive oil
2 sprigs rosemary
Fine salt to taste
Black pepper to taste

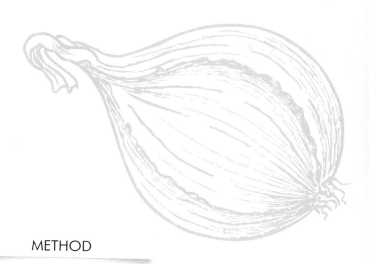

METHOD

Cook the pasta in plenty of boiling salted water.
When cooked, drain and leave to cool.
Peel and wash the vegetables.
Cut the celery, carrots and onion into 2 mm cubes.
Put two tablespoons of olive oil into a frying pan, add the chopped vegetables, cover and cook over a medium heat. Season with salt.
Puree the beans and season the puree with salt and pepper.
Put the bean puree into a piping bag and fill the mezze maniche, one by one.
Put the bread crumbs in the bottom of a baking dish, cover with the vegetables and the filled pasta.
Finish with another layer of vegetables and a generous sprinkling of grated cheese.
Put in the oven at 200° C and bake until golden.

SPAGHETTI WITH EGGS AND PEAS

SERVES **4**

3 whole eggs
100 g "00" flour
100 g Grana Padano cheese
200 g peas, pureed and passed
through a sieve

100 g boiled peas
Fine salt to taste
Black pepper to taste
30 g extra virgin olive oil
2 l vegetable stock

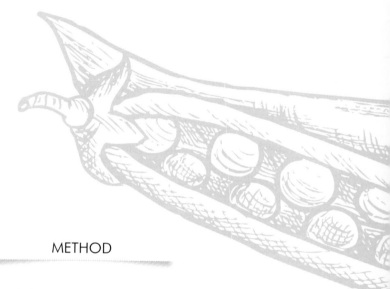

METHOD

Mix the eggs vigorously with the pea puree in a bowl.
Add the flour, 70 g of grated cheese and mix well.
Season with salt.
Leave the mixture to stand in the refrigerator over night, to allow the pasta to become elastic.
Put the mixture into a pastry bag and cut an opening with a diameter of 3-4 mm, squeeze the mixture into the simmering stock; cook the pasta for 2 minutes and drain well.
Serve the pasta in a bowl with a little oil, boiled peas, freshly ground pepper and a sprinkling of grated cheese.

PASTA PIE WITH MOZZARELLA, ASPARAGUS AND TRUFFLE SAUCE

SERVES 4

280 g egg pasta
250 g mozzarella
2 sprigs thyme
150 g breadcrumbs
Black truffle or truffle paste to taste
4 g corn starch
500 g wild asparagus

4 tbsp extra virgin olive oil
1 onion
2 sprigs parsley
20 g butter
4 individual moulds
400 ml stock made with asparagus stalks
Fine salt to taste

METHOD

Cook the pasta in plenty of boiling salted water.
Melt the butter in a pan and butter the moulds well with a brush, then sprinkling them with breadcrumbs.
Cut the mozzarella into thin slices.
Wash and clean the asparagus and break them by hand, removing the tip from the hard and fibrous bottom part of the stem. Use the hard part to make the stock.
Put two tablespoons of olive oil into a frying pan, add the chopped onion and asparagus, cover and cook on a low heat.
Now prepare the sauce by dissolving the cornstarch in a little water and then adding it to the stock, add the remaining oil, the truffle paste and chopped parsley.
Cook for at least 4-5 minutes, until it begins to thicken.
Drain the pasta, cut coarsely and toss in a bowl with the mozzarella and chopped thyme.
Fill the moulds with the dressed pasta.
Preheat the oven and bake for 7-8 minutes at 180° C.
Once they are ready, place the soup in the bottom of the dish, then the pasta pie and place the warm asparagus on top.

CANNELLONCINI CRÊPES WITH RICOTTA AND HAZELNUTS

SERVES **4**

4 crêpes*
500 g cow's milk ricotta
200 g hazelnuts
Nutmeg to taste

100 g grated cheese
250 ml béchamel*
Melted butter to taste
Truffle shavings

METHOD

Grind the hazelnuts to a powder in a kitchen machine.
Pass the ricotta through a sieve into a bowl, add the hazelnut powder, nutmeg, salt and mix well.
Leave the mixture to rest in the refrigerator for 4 hours.
Take the crêpes, cut them in half and fill them with the ricotta mixture.
Roll up the crêpes to the size of a cigar and cut each cylinder thus obtained into three parts.
Brush a baking dish with melted butter, arrange the cannelloncini in the dish, dot with the remainder of the butter and sprinkle with grated cheese.
Bake at 180° C for 35 minutes.
Now take the béchamel sauce you have prepared in a saucepan off the heat and add the Parmesan cheese.
Put the hot sauce into a dish, place the cannelloncini on top of it and finish with truffle shavings.

BLACK BEADS WITH CLAMS, COLOURFUL VEGETABLES AND MOZZARELLA

SERVES 4

250 g pre-cooked couscous
270 ml water
2 sachets of cuttlefish ink
400 g mussels
1 clove garlic
100 g courgettes

100 g tinned peas
4 sprigs parsley
130 g mozzarella
5 tbsp extra virgin olive oil
Fine salt to taste

METHOD

Wash and cut the courgettes into cubes.
Place the courgettes into a bowl, season with a pinch of salt and a tablespoon of olive oil and saute in the frying pan over a high heat. When cooked, add the peas.
Put two tablespoons of olive oil and the garlic into a frying pan.
Heat, add the mussels and cover.
As soon as the mussels have opened, turn off the heat, shell them and keep aside the cooking water.
Put the water, the cooking water of the mussels, squid ink, two tablespoons of olive oil, a teaspoon of salt into a saucepan and bring to the boil.
Sprinkle the cous cous into the pan and turn off the heat. Leave it to sit for a few minutes and separate the grains of the couscous with a fork. Cover with a lid.
When it is ready, add the mussels and vegetables to the cous cous.
Mix well. It is important that the ingredients are either all hot or all cold.
Serve with mozarella and chopped parsley on top of the cous cous.

RISOTTO WITH ROASTED CHICKEN, PIAVE CHEESE AND PROSECCO

SERVES **4**

280 **g** Vialone nano rice
2 glasses Prosecco
100 **g** onion
2 **l** vegetable stock
½ roast chicken
2 sprigs rosemary

4 sage leaves
2 **tbsp** mustard
40 **g** butter
100 **g** mature Piave cheese
Fine salt to taste
Black pepper to taste

METHOD

Chop the onion finely and sauté in a frying pan with 20 g of butter and ½ glass white wine until it becomes translucent.
Put the butter in a saucepan, melt and add the rice.
Cook for two minutes, stirring well.
When the rice becomes translucent, pour in a glass of Prosecco and allow it to evaporate.
Add the cooked onion.
Continue cooking, adding a little stock at a time.
Meanwhile, dice the roast chicken.
Place the roast chicken in a non-stick frying pan and fry.
Add the chopped herbs, mustard and a splash of Prosecco and let it evaporate.
Cook for about 15 minutes then remove the risotto from the heat, add the butter and let it melt, stirring well. Add the grated cheese and black pepper. Mix well.
Place a scoop of rice in the dish, place the chicken on top, drizzle with olive oil and sprinkle with pepper.

SCALDED SOUP WITH CHICKEN AND FENNEL

SERVES 4

1 l chicken stock*
½ boiled chicken
20 g flour
6 tbsp extra virgin olive oil

1 fennel bulb
24 sunflower seeds
Fine salt to taste

METHOD

Prepare a good stock, filter it and remove the fat.
Bone the chicken and cut it into small pieces.
Put two tablespoons of olive oil in a frying pan, add the chicken and fry over a
high heat. Season with salt.
Mix 2 tablespoons of olive oil with the flour in a saucepan and cook for a few
minutes over low heat until it turns light brown.
Add the hot stock to the preparation of oil and flour a little at a time, stirring
with a whisk.
Cook until it has a creamy consistency.
Wash the fennel and cut it into small cubes.
Add them to the broth at the last moment as they should be warm and crispy.
Put the hot broth onto a dish, then the browned chicken, the fennel fronds that
you have kept aside and a drizzle of olive oil.

RISOTTO WITH SAUSAGE, ENDIVE AND RED WINE REDUCTION

SERVES **4**

280 g Carnaroli rice
50 g butter
1 cup white wine
250 g sausage
Extra virgin olive oil to taste
250 g Belgian endive

1 l beef stock*
Fine salt to taste
100 g grated Parmesan cheese
1 cup red wine
2 tbsp sugar

METHOD

Place the red wine and sugar in a small saucepan.
Cook over a low heat until the wine is reduced. Keep to one side.
Put 20 g butter and the rice in a saucepan and cook over a medium heat until the rice becomes translucent.
Add half a cup of white wine and let it evaporate.
Continue cooking, adding a little stock at a time.
Cook for about 15 minutes, stirring occasionally.
Meanwhile, remove the sausage casing and crumble the meat into a bowl with ½ glass of wine.
Put the sausage with the wine in a frying pan, cover and fry on a medium heat.
Wash, peel and cut the endive into thin strips (julienne).
Put the endive into a bowl and season with salt and oil.
Sear the endive in a frying pan. Keep it warm.
When the rice is almost cooked, add the sausages and turn off the heat.
Add the butter, grated cheese and incorporate well into the risotto.
Place the seared endive and a scoop of risotto in a dish and drizzle over the red wine reduction.

BLACK AND WHITE RISOTTO

SERVES 4

250 g Arborio rice
40 g shallots
400 g cleaned cuttlefish
5 g cuttlefish ink
30 g butter

50 g grated Parmesan cheese
4 sprigs parsley
1 glass dry white wine
4 tbsp extra virgin olive oil
2 l fish stock*

METHOD

Dice the cuttlefish.
Chop the shallots, put them in a saucepan with the oil and the cuttlefish, cook over a moderate heat.
Cook until golden brown then add the rice.
When the rice becomes translucent, pour in a glass of Prosecco and allow it to evaporate.
Once evaporated, continue cooking, adding a little boiling stock at a time.
When the rice is almost cooked, turn off the heat, add the butter and the grated cheese and mix well.
Put half of the rice straight into another saucepan, add the cuttlefish ink and stir.
Put a spoonful of white rice alongside a spoonful of black rice onto a dish.
Finish by sprinkling with chopped parsley.

FRIED RICE WITH RED BEANS AND EGGS

SERVES **4**

250 g boiled rice
3 sage leaves
40 g butter
250 g boiled red beans
150 g celery

150 g carrots
4 eggs
Fine salt to taste
1/2 cup white wine vinegar

METHOD

Put the butter and sage into a frying pan, when the butter is melted and well
seasoned, add the boiled rice and fry.
Wash, peel and chop the celery and carrots.
Put the already cooked beans into a saucepan then add the chopped celery and
carrots and sautee for a few minutes until the vegetables are tender but crisp.
Keep to one side.
Now prepare the poached egg: Put the water, salt and vinegar into a saucepan.
Break the egg onto a saucer.
When the water has almost come to the boil, stir it creating a vortex and
pout the egg into the centre. Cook for a few minutes until the egg white has
solidified but the yolk is still soft.
Remove the egg with a slotted spoon and place it on a sheet of absorbent paper.
Repeat with the other eggs.
To assemble the dish, place the rice in the centre of the plate, put the sauteed beans
and vegetables around it and, finally, place the poached egg on top of the rice.
Drizzle olive oil over the egg and sprinkle with freshly ground pepper.

BARLEY AND AROMATIC BORLOTTI BEANS WITH ROOT VEGETABLES

SERVES **4**

160 **g** pearl barley
250 **g** cooked borlotti beans
40 **g** butter
2 sage leaves
3 sprigs rosemary

20 **g** onions
80 **g** rye bread
150 **g** white turnips, radishes and carrots
80 **g** grated cheese
Fine salt to taste

METHOD

Toast the rye bread in the oven and chop. Keep to one side.
Chop the sage, rosemary and onion.
Put the butter, the chopped rosemary, sage and onion into a saucepan.
Fry gently.
Add the barley and cover with water.
Bring to the boil then cook for another 30 minutes.
Add the beans.
Chop the turnips, radishes, carrots, add them to the beans and cook for a further 3-4 minutes.
Turn off the heat, add the butter and Parmesan. Mix well.
Put a spoonful of barley and beans in a dish and sprinkle with rye bread.

SPAGHETTI WITH SOUTHERN PESTO AND AUBERGINE

SERVES **4**

280 **g** spaghetti
FOR THE SOUTHERN PESTO
4 sprigs parsley
15 **g** basil leaves
½ level tsp oregano
7 desalted capers
½ small clove garlic
½ fresh chilli
40g celery

125 **g** tomato slices*
2 **g** fine salt
50 **g** extra virgin olive oil
FOR THE PASTA GARNICH
400 **g** aubergine
1 clove garlic
2 **tbsp** extra virgin olive oil
200 **g** tomato slices*
Fine salt to taste

METHOD

For the southern pesto: Put the well chilled ingredients in a food processor: parsley, basil, white celery (heart), garlic, capers, oregano, red pepper and tomato slices.
Finally add the salt and the oil. Blend all the ingredients to give a rustic mixture.
For the pasta garnish: Cut the tomato slices into small cubes and toss with the salt. Partially peel the aubergine removing some strips of skin with a potato peeler. Cut the aubergine into cubes and saute in the frying pan with a clove of garlic and olive oil.
To complete the dish: Cook the pasta, drain it in a bowl, toss with the southern pesto, place on plates and sprinkle with the diced aubergine and tomatoes.

RICE AND LENTIL SOUP
WITH SEARED PIG'S FEET

SERVES **4**

1 pork sausage
300 g cooked lentils
200 g celery, carrots, onion
100 g boiled rice

100 g choux pastry*
3 tbsp extra virgin olive oil
Fine salt to taste

METHOD

Peel and wash the carrots, celery and onion.
Cut the vegetables into cubes of 2 mm by 2 mm.
Put the oil into a saucepan, add the vegetables and fry gently.
Add the cooked lentils, season with salt and cook. Keep warm.
Mix the cold boiled rice with the cold choux pastry in a bowl.
When the mixture is blended well, put it into a piping bag.
Lightly grease a baking sheet, pipe strips with the dough.
Sprinkle with water and bake at 180° C for about 10 minutes.
When cooked, cut the strips into pieces.
To serve put a spoonful of lentils, bits of choux and rice and two slices of
sausage per person in a dish.

PASTA WITH BACON, BROAD BEANS AND CACIOCAVALLO CHEESE

SERVES 4

300 g wholemeal pasta
250 g bacon
½ glass white wine
400 g shelled fresh broad beans

12 mint leaves
400 g tomato
200 g caciocavallo cheese
Fine salt to taste

METHOD

Cook the pasta in boiling salted water in a saucepan.
Cut the bacon into thin strips, put it into a bowl and marinate in the white wine for about an hour.
Put the bacon in a frying pan without oil, cover and fry over a low heat.
Blanch the broad beans in boiling water, shell them, put them in a bowl and flavour them with mint.
Wash the tomatoes, score a cross on the bottom and put in boiling water, leaving them immersed for fifteen seconds, then cool them quickly by dipping them in water and ice.
Drain them again. Now, remove the skin, which will come away easily. Cut the tomatoes into four, removing the core and seeds.
This will give you tomato slices.
Bake in an oven at 90° C for 40 minutes and then cut into small wedges.
Finally, drain the pasta and toss with the bacon, add the blanched beans and tomato. Stir well and garnish the pasta with the cheese cut into strips.

PASTA SALAD WITH CHICKPEAS AND COD

SERVES 4

200 g pasta
300 g dried salted codfish
250 g cherry tomatoes
60 g fresh onion
200 g boiled chickpeas

3 sprigs parsley
1 fresh chilli
Fine salt to taste
2 tbsp extra virgin olive oil

METHOD

Cook the pasta in a large pot of boiling salted water.
Cut the cod into pieces and toss with oil.
Grill starting with the skin side down.
Put the tomatoes cut into quarters, the onion and the chopped chilli into a
bowl. Season with salt and two tablespoons of olive oil.
Fry the tomatoes in a frying pan.
Add the chickpeas and chopped parsley.
Drain the pasta and put it into the tomato and chick peas, stir well.
Serve the pasta in a dish with the salt cod shredded by hand on top and add a
drizzle of extra virgin olive oil.

PASTA BAKE WITH SAN DANIELE HAM, MUSHROOMS AND PEAS

INGREDIENTS FOR **1** RING MOULD

500 g spaghetti
8 slices ham
500 g peas
1 white onion
600 g button mushrooms
100 g Montasio cheese, grated

4 egg yolks
50 g butter
40 g "00" flour
¼ l vegetable broth*
Extra virgin olive oil
Fine salt to taste

METHOD

Break the spaghetti in half and cook them along with the peas in lightly salted boiling water.

Clean and wash the mushrooms. Cut them first in half and then into slices.

Chop the onion and fry in a frying pan with two tablespoons of olive oil and the mushrooms.

Cover and cook on a medium heat. Season with salt.

When the mushrooms are cooked, add the broth.

Separately, melt the butter in a small saucepan, when melted, add the flour and mix well.

Cook for a few minutes and add the mixture to the mushrooms.

Once the pasta is cooked, drain and toss in the pan with the mushrooms, remove from the heat and add the grated cheese and the egg yolks.

Line the inside of a ring mould with slices of ham.

Put the pasta mixture in the ring mould.

Bake for 40 minutes at 150° C.

Leave to stand before turning the ring over on a serving plate.

AUBERGINE AND RICOTTA ROLLS WITH BASIL, PINE NUTS AND TOMATO SAUCE

SERVES 4

1 **kg** aubergines
200 **g** small pasta tubes
400 **g** ricotta
10 basil leaves
60 **g** pine nuts

80 **g** grated cheese
300 **g** tomato sauce*
4 **tbsp** extra virgin olive oil
Fine salt to taste

METHOD

Wash the aubergines and remove some strips of peel lengthwise with a potato peeler.

Cut the aubergine into 1 cm slices width wise.

Place a piece of parchment on a baking tray, brush the aubergines with oil on both sides and roast in the oven at 220° C until golden brown (about 10 minutes). Remove from the oven and add salt.

Coarsely chop the basil only when you are ready to use it. Mix the basil with the ricotta, grated cheese, pine nuts and chopped coarsely. Season with salt.

Separately, boil the pasta, drain when cooked, toss with 5 g of oil and leave to cool. Add the cold pasta to the seasoned ricotta and stir well.

Put the ricotta mixture and pasta in a piping bag.

Now, make the rolls by piping the ricotta onto a slice of aubergine, roll up, then place the roll on an oiled baking tray with the end part down.

Cover the rolls with tomato sauce and grated cheese.

Bake at 180° C for 10 minutes. When cooked, wait 10 minutes before serving.

BUCATINI WITH PECORINO, PRAWNS AND ASPARAGUS

SERVES **4**

350 g bucatini
200 g borage
200 g wild asparagus
600 g prawns
120 g Pecorino cheese

4 tbsp extra virgin olive oil
100 ml concentrated fish stock
Black pepper to taste
Fine salt to taste

METHOD

Clean the prawns and cut them into small pieces.
Put them in a bowl and season with salt.
Keep aside in the refrigerator for two hours covered with plastic wrap.
Meanwhile, cook the pasta in plenty of salted water.
Wash the asparagus and remove the toughest part of the stem. Cut them into small pieces.
Put the oil into a saucepan and sauté the asparagus.
Peel and wash the borage.
When the pasta has cooked for 6 minutes, put the borage into the water and cook together.
Add the prawns to the asparagus, keep the heat low, cover and cook for about 2 minutes.
Add the concentrated fish stock, bring back to the boil.
Drain the pasta with borage and pour it into the pan with the asparagus and prawns, stir.
Add the cheese into which you have previously ground the black pepper, remove the saucepan from the heat, cover and leave to stand for two minutes, then stir and serve.

BREAD SOUP WITH VEGETABLES AND EGG AU GRATIN

SERVES **4**

4 slices (**350 g**) stale bread
600 g minestrone soup*
4 eggs

150 g grated mature cheese
Extra virgin olive oil to taste
Fine salt to taste

METHOD

Cut the bread into 1 cm slices and put it in the refrigerator.
Toast the bread in the oven at 200° C for 3-4 minutes.
Break each egg into a saucer.
Take 4 earthenware casserole dishes and make layers, as follows:
a slice of bread in the bottom, the soup, grated cheese, raw egg, more cheese
and a drizzle of oil.
Bake at 220° C until the top of the dish is golden brown.
Serve hot or cold.

RISOTTO WITH RADICCHIO AND STRACCIATELLA ALLA ROMANA

SERVES 4

240 g superfine Carnaroli rice
10 g butter
1 l vegetable stock
200 ml dry white wine

FOR THE RADICCHIO
200 g radicchio
20 g extra virgin olive oil
Fine salt to taste
30 g "Maturata" onion (already cooked in oil or butter and wine)

FOR THE STRACCIATELLA
100 g water
20 g lemon juice
Fine salt to taste
1 whole egg
2 egg yolks
40 g Pecorino Romano cheese
1 sprig parsley
Black pepper to taste
Lemon zest to flavour

TO MIX
40 g Pecorino Romano cheese

METHOD

For the radicchio: Clean the radicchio, dry it well, cut coarsely and place in a bowl. Season with salt, olive oil and stir.
Spread it evenly in a saucepan and let it simmer over a medium heat with the lid on.
For the stracciatella: Combine the egg and egg yolks, Pecorino cheese, chopped parsley, grated lemon zest and black pepper.
Put the water, lemon juice and salt in a saucepan and bring to the boil.
Beat the mixture well and add it to the flavoured hot water. Continue cooking for 1 minute, then turn off the heat. Leave it to cook until it forms a stracciatella. Pass through the chinois strainer and let it drain well.
For the risotto: Put the butter in a saucepan, add the rice and toast.
Add the "maturata" onion and cover with ¾ of the wine, let the wine evaporate. Cook over a medium heat, adding the vegetable stock from time to time. Halfway through cooking, add the stewed radicchio and the remaining dry white wine and continue cooking the rice.
It is important that the radicchio is warm when it is added to the rice as it is cooking. When cooked, remove from the heat and stir the rice, finally add the grated Pecorino. Serve the risotto sprinkled with the stracciatella.

CHARD BUNDLES WITH EGGS AU GRATIN

SERVES **4**

8 crepes*
300 g ricotta
300 g boiled chard
1 egg
2 tbsp milk
Sesame seeds to taste

100 g white bread crumbs
Grated cheese to taste
400 g red tomatoes
5 basil leaves
Fine salt to taste

METHOD

Make a centrifuge with tomato, basil and salt. Keep to one side.
Squeeze the chard well and chop coarsely.
Mix the ricotta with salt and grated cheese in a bowl.
Open the crepes on a table, sprinkle with ricotta and arrange the chard on top.
Roll the crepes into bundles and arrange in a buttered casserole dish.
Beat the egg with a little milk, brush on the crepes and sprinkle with sesame
seeds and bread crumbs.
Leave to rest in the fridge and repeat the operation with the milk, sesame seeds
and bread three times before baking at 170° C for 15 minutes.
Put the tomato centrifuge in a bowl, lay the crepes on top and serve.

MEAT, FISH & MORE

TERRINE OF CHICKEN WITH MUSCAT WINE

SERVES **6/8**

1 whole boned chicken
25 thin slices fatty bacon
½ l Muscat wine
Fine salt to taste
200 g minced veal
200 g diced pork
100 g sliced bread, crusts removed

1 whole egg
Milk as required (To soak the bread)
6 carrot sticks (decoration)
Nutmeg to taste
6 small gherkins
Ready-made chicken stock

METHOD

Clean the boned chicken well and singe it slightly to remove the feathers.
Wash the skin thoroughly with a little vinegar, then dry well. Put the chicken to
marinate in the Muscat wine for at least 8 hours adding a little salt.
After marinating, place a sheet of parchment paper on a flat surface and cover it
with thin slices of bacon. Separately, dry the marinated chicken and beat with a
meat tenderiser, then place it on the "bed" of bacon.
Meanwhile, prepare a mixture with the finely chopped meat, the sliced bread
soaked in milk, egg, salt and a little nutmeg. If possible, pass the mixture
through a meat grinder to make it as smooth as possible.
Place 2/3 of the mixture inside the tenderised chicken in a width wise direction
(not lengthwise, as is done classically). Take care to go to the edges.
Arrange the carrot sticks and gherkins on top of the mixture also in a width
wise direction. Lightly press the ingredients into the mixture, then cover them
with the remaining meat mixture.
Close the chicken tightly on itself once again in the direction of the width of
the chicken, starting from the breast. When it is rolled up, make sure the edges
of the parchment paper are closed well and place the roll in a terrine mould
(about 25 cm long). Flatten to make it take the shape of the mould.
Wrap it in plastic wrap and perforate the surface lightly with a toothpick.
Put a braising pan on the heat and place the mould inside it, fill with water up
to the middle of the mould. Bake in a covered water bath for about an hour and
a half. Leave to cool first at room temperature, compressing the chicken terrine
with a weight. Then store it in the refrigerator.
This dish should be served sliced and cold with a side dish of pickled vegetables.

TERRINE OF COD WITH BLACK OLIVES IN A LEEK NET

SERVES **6/8**

1 leek
500 g desalted cod
50 g extra virgin olive oil
150 g white onion
250 ml milk

140 ml water
1 egg white
100 g pitted black olives
Fine salt to taste

METHOD

Slice the desalted cod, put in a saucepan, add 125 ml milk and 70 ml water then cook for about 10 minutes to completely desalt.

Drain the cod after 10 minutes, add the oil, finely sliced onion, an additional 250 ml of milk and 250 ml of water to the saucepan and continue with the final cooking.

Cover and continue cooking over a low heat. It is also important to sauté it a little, once you have drained it from the milk and water.

When cooked, blend it all in the mixer, add the egg white and oil in a stream. Finally add the black olives to the mixture. Keep to one side.

Meanwhile, boil the leaves of the leek in boiling salted water. Drain well, pat dry, cut into strips 1.5 cm wide and weave the leaves, as if to form a net, which you then place in the bottom of the previously buttered terrine mould.

Use a piping bag to pipe the cod and olive mixture into the terrine, use a wet spoon to level and compact the mixture, making sure there are no air bubbles. Then cover the top with blanched leek leaves. Dot the top of the terrine with 30 g of butter, which will melt gradually in the oven and protect the terrine during cooking.

Bake the dish in a preheated oven at 120° C for about 35 minutes. Serve the terrine hot, cut into slices with blanched vegetables and dressed with balsamic glaze or vinegar.

AMBERJACK AND BORLOTTI BEAN PIE WITH SAUTEED FENNEL

SERVES 4

200 g amberjack fillet
200 g cooked borlotti beans
15 g chives
3 tbsp extra virgin olive oil
10 g mixed fresh herbs

2 egg yolks
2 egg whites
Salt and pepper to taste
250 g fresh fennel

METHOD

Season the amberjack with salt, pepper and 1 tablespoon oil.
Sear it on a griddle or in a frying pan for a few minutes, then put it in the oven to finish cooking. Keep it aside to cool.
Blend the beans and the amberjack in a blender and then pass through a sieve, put everything in a bowl and season with salt and chopped chives. Stir in the egg yolks and set aside.
Beat the egg whites until stiff, then incorporate the mixture being careful not to remove the air, to do this use a slotted spoon or a whisk and stir very slowly from the bottom upwards.
Butter the ramekins / bowls and fill to 3/4 full with the mixture.
Preheat the oven to 175° C with steam and put the ramekins in to cook for 5 minutes, then finish the cooking in a dry oven at 160° C for another 10 minutes.
Serve the pies with a salad of fennel, oranges and olives, which brings the right amount of freshness to the dish.

PROVOLONE CHEESE FLAN WITH PEARS IN RED WINE

SERVES **4**

250 g shortcrust pastry
200 g Provolone cheese cubes
One tsp curry powder
50 g butter
50 g flour
250 ml milk

3 egg yolks
3 egg whites
2 pears
250 ml dry red wine
100 g granulated sugar
Salt to taste

METHOD

For the pears: Wash the pears, peel and cut into cubes.
Place them in the bottom of a saucepan, cover with wine and sugar, and cook over a gentle heat until the wine is thick, assuming the consistency of a syrup.
For the flan: Infuse the milk in a bowl with the curry.
Roll out the shortcrust pastry to a thickness of about 4 mm and line a loaf tin which has been previously buttered and floured.
Make a roux with the butter and flour: melt the butter over the fire, then, remove from the heat, add the flour all at once, return to the heat and continue to stir and cook until it turns golden.
Remove the roux from the heat and add the milk all at once, stirring quickly with a whisk to avoid lumps.
Return to the heat and continue cooking on a low heat for at least 10 minutes, add salt. When the mixture reaches a firm consistency and comes away from the sides of the pan, remove it from the heat and leave to stand for 5 minutes. Then, stir in the egg yolks vigorously with a spoon and finally add the diced Provolone.
Beat the egg whites but do not make them too stiff then add them in two lots to the mixture stirring gently from the bottom upwards with a slotted spoon.
Pour the mixture into the lined mould and bake in a preheated oven at 185° C for the first 10 minutes, then lower the heat to 165° C until the end of cooking.
Once cooked, turn the flan out of the mould, slice and serve with the pears in red wine.

COURGETTE AND RICOTTA FLAN

SERVES **6**

300 g courgettes
30 g butter
2 egg yolks
125 g ricotta

50 g grated parmesan cheese
40 g corn starch
Salt and pepper to taste

METHOD

Wash, peel and slice the courgettes. Place them in a frying pan with a knob of butter and a little salt, cover and cook.

Separately, combine the ricotta, courgettes, grated cheese and starch in a saucepan then put on the heat and cook over a low heat, stir constantly on the heat until the mixture becomes a thick cream. Leave to stand for a few minutes off the heat then stir in the egg yolks vigorously with a spoon. Season the mixture with salt and pepper.

Beat the egg whites until stiff, then incorporate the mixture being careful not to remove the air, to do this use a slotted spoon or a whisk and stir very slowly from the bottom upwards.

Butter the ramekins and fill 3/4 full with the mixture.

Bake at 120° C in water bath, or place the moulds on a high baking tray cover with a cloth and then fill the tray with water to three quarters full for 20-25 minutes. Serve the flan warm when freshly baked.

MEDALLION OF CHICORY, POTATOES AND BROAD BEANS WITH SAUTÉED LAMB AND WILD ONIONS

SERVES **4**

400 g lamb (pulp)
2 layers dried tomatoes,
150 g boiled chicory
100 g boiled new potatoes
150 g dried broad beans

150 g wild onions
Marjoram, to taste
4 tbsp extra virgin olive oil
2 tbsp chilli oil
Fine salt, to taste

METHOD

Put the diced lamb in a bowl and season with salt and marjoram.
Marinate for 12 hours in the refrigerator, covered with plastic wrap.
Leave the broad beans to rehydrate for 4-6 hours.
After this time, pan fry the meat with some oil over a high heat, with the lid. Do not turn it until it is browned and continue cooking.
Put the oil in a pan with the chopped dried tomatoes, the chicory and the coarsely diced potatoes. Leave it to cook.
Rinse the broad beans and toss them in a pan with spices of your choice, salt and add them to the chicory.
Lay out the dish to form a medallion of chicory, with the aid of a pasta bowl, put the lamb on top and the wild onions dressed with chilli oil on the sides.

MEATBALLS WITH PISTACHIO AND SESAME WITH PIZZAIOLA TOMATO SAUCE AND POTATO CHIPS

SERVES **4**

300 **g** minced veal
100 **g** bread Loaf chopped (no crust)
4 sprigs parsley
1 egg
100 **g** flour and water batter*
Chopped pistachios, as needed

60 **g** green olives
1 garlic
4 **g** oregano
300 **g** tomato sauce
80 **g** extra virgin olive oil
200 **g** potatoes

METHOD

Chop the olives into small pieces.

Put the oil, olives and crushed garlic In a saucepan. Fry.

Add the oregano, salt and tomato sauce.

Cook without a lid until the sauce has thickened.

Combine in a bowl the chopped parsley, egg, minced meat, sifted white bread and mix well.

Form the meatballs, roll them in the batter and then in the chopped pistachios.

Peel and cut the potatoes into chips. Keep them in cold water. Drain and dry well.

Deep-fry in oil the potatoes first and then the meatballs.

Lay out the dish with red sauce on the bottom, then the meatballs and potato chips on top.

MINI POCKETS OF PORK
TO THE MEMORY OF TYROL

SERVES 4

600 g pork loin
200 g loaf of Bread (without crust)
6 slices air-cured pork meat
30 g onion
60 g cold butter
2 sprigs parsley
1 glass white wine

Juice of 1 lemon
Fine salt, to taste
Black pepper, to taste
"00" flour, as needed
4 tbsp extra virgin olive oil
Toothpicks

METHOD

Chop the onion.
Sauté the onion in a saucepan with 30 g of butter.
Add the air-cured pork meat cut into strips. Leave to cool.
In the blender, grind the bread and add the mirepoix, making the filling of the mini pockets. Cut the pork into about 2 cm thick slices, remove the connective tissue, not suitable for fast cooking, and with a pointed knife, make a slit as to form pockets.
Fill them with the mixture of bread, mirepoix and pork loin, without adding extra salt, and hold the meat with a toothpick.
Salt the pockets on both sides, flour lightly and cook them in a pan with oil.
Deglaze the gravy with wine, butter, lemon juice and chopped parsley, using it as a sauce to go with it.
Once ready, serve the pockets with vegetables on the side like broccoli or Brussels sprouts.

UNUSUAL TUNA WITH RED WINE REDUCTION AND SWEET AND SOUR SAUCE

SERVES 4

600 g fresh tuna slices
8 slices lard
120 g courgettes
120 g peppers
120 g aubergines
8 g oregano

Fine salt, to taste
5 tbsp extra virgin olive oil
300 g sweet and sour sauce*
For the red wine reduction:
750 ml red wine
200 g sugar

METHOD

Place the wine and sugar in a saucepan and let it reduce on a moderate heat until it reaches an oily consistency.

Cut the vegetables into cubes, ½ cm per side. In a bowl, season them with salt, oregano and olive oil.

Cook the vegetables in a casserole with the lid.

Cut the tuna into four fillets, salted on both sides.

Arrange around each filet two slices of bacon, tying them with string.

Scald the tuna on the griddle, for 4-5 minutes.

The lard should be crisp.

Put the tuna in the centre of a large bowl next to a bowl with the red wine reduction. Next to this place the sweet and sour sauce and stewed vegetables.

Serve with a drizzle of olive oil and a sprinkling of pepper.

SCAMPI WITH PROSECCO AND POLENTA WITH SPICY SAUCE

SERVES **4**

12 scampi
1 glass of Prosecco
3 sprigs parsley
4 tbsp extra virgin olive oil
400 g Polenta*

FOR THE CURRY SAUCE
1 tbsp curry
100 g yellow bell pepper
200 ml fresh cream

FOR THE SPICY PRAWN SAUCE
Shrimp heads
1 white onion
2 cloves garlic
4 sprigs parsley
1 glass of Prosecco
5 g chilli powder
400 g peeled tomatoes

METHOD

Shell the prawns, keep the tails and heads.

Put some oil in a saucepan with the prawn heads and fry.

Add the onion, garlic and chopped parsley, cover with the lid and continue cooking.

When everything is nicely browned, pour 1 glass of wine, let it evaporate, then add the chilli, tomato and a glass of water.

Cook for at least 30 minutes with the lid on until the sauce is thick.

Strain the sauce, season with salt and set aside.

Make a sauce to accompany the dish by whipping the fresh cream, curry and yellow bell pepper.

In a small saucepan, put 1 glass of wine, 3 sprigs of parsley, salt and a little olive oil.

When it starts to make smoke, gently add the prawns. It should not boil because the cooking must be gentle and short to maintain the pulp soft. Drain the prawns.

On the bottom of the plate put the hot sauce over the polenta, scampi and lastly a few drops of curry sauce with a little olive oil.

VEAL ROLLS WITH CHEESE OF RAGUSA AND BREADCRUMBS WITH OREGANO

SERVES **4**

8 slices steer
Sage, to taste
200 g sifted white bread
200 g finely diced Ragusano cheese
Oregano, to taste
1 egg

FOR THE ACCOMPANYING SAUCE
100 g olives
5 sprigs parsley
6 blanched almonds
1 red garlic
6 tbsp extra virgin olive oil
Fine salt, to taste

METHOD

Make the filling of the rolls, mixing well in a bowl the bread with the cheese, egg and a bit of oregano.

Arrange the slices of meat on a flat surface, flatten them and place on each slice a spoonful of the mixture, then making it into a roll.

Fill the rolls two at a time, turning the opening on the inner side, and interspersing with a sage leaf.

Close with large toothpicks and sprinkle with a little oil helping yourself with your hands.

Add salt and roll them in the sifted white bread with chopped parsley.

Grill them slowly on both sides.

Put the olives, almonds, garlic and oil in a blender. Blend them coarsely. Season with salt.

Serve the rolls accompanied by the olive and almond sauce.

CODFISH WITH CHESTNUTS, HAM AND POTATO SLICES

SERVES **4**

4 slices of raw ham
4 slices of desalted cod
3 white onions
1 l milk
1 l Water
1 bay leaf

200 g boiled chestnuts
4 sprigs parsley
400 g boiled potatoes cut into round into slices
5 tbsp extra virgin olive oil

METHOD

Julienne the onions and arrange them on the bottom of a casserole dish with oil. Lay on the bed of onions the slices of codfish.

When the onions begin to brown, pour the milk to cover the slices and the water; add the bay leaf and cook over a low heat with the lid on for at least 1 hour.

After this time, remove the lid to dry the liquid, add the chestnuts and chopped parsley.

Let it dry to make a cream.

Serve the cod with a slice of ham on top, accompanied with boiled potatoes with parsley.

TERRINE OF AUBERGINE AND WHITE FISH WITH DRIED TOMATOES

INGREDIENTS FOR 1 TERRINE

500 g grilled aubergines
300 g flesh of white fish (e.g. Cod, haddock)
3 egg whites
200 g loaf of bread (without crust)

½ cup fresh cream
3 dried tomatoes
3 capers
2 sprigs parsley
Fine salt, to taste

METHOD

Chop the flesh of the fish and put it in a blender with the egg whites, bread and salt. Blend and add the cream.

Put the mixture in a bowl and add the dried tomatoes, capers and parsley, all coarsely chopped, mix well.

Line a baking tin with greaseproof paper and with the grilled aubergines, covering well the sides of the tin (the aubergines will seal the sides).

Fill the tin with the fish mixture.

Close it with the aubergines from the sides, the parchment paper and seal with plastic wrap.

Then lay it in a terracotta bowl with cold water and cook in a water bath for 1 hour at 90°C.

Let it cool and put it in the tin, still closed, to rest in the fridge overnight. Turn it out and serve cold.

ENDIVE IN VEAL WITH TUNA SAUCE

SERVES **4**

1 kg whole sirloin meat
20 g mustard sauce
2 sprigs rosemary
300 g endive
Fine salt, to taste

FOR THE SAUCE
250 g low-fat plain yogurt
200 g tuna in olive oil
3 boiled egg yolks
3 anchovy filets
3 sprigs parsley
Fine salt, to taste

METHOD

Take the entire piece of meat, salt it, and rub it to help it dissolve.
Then rub it with mustard, about 2 tablespoons per side. Rub evenly.
Cover the meat with the rosemary sprigs and tie with string, not too tight, just to give it shape.
Bake at a low temperature until it gets to 54°C at the core.
Turn up the oven to 200°C for the last 10 minutes.
Peel the endive, cut into six pieces lengthwise. Season with salt and oil and grill it.
Prepare the sauce by putting in a food processor the yoghurt, tuna, well drained from the oil, egg yolks, anchovies and parsley, blend well until you get a smooth sauce.
Cut the roast beef into thin slices, place the endive in the centre and wrap it in the meat like a roulade.
Put three rolls on each plate and drizzle with the tuna sauce and freshly chopped parsley.

STEWED BEEF IN RED WINE

SERVES **4**

600 g steer riblets
150 g celery, carrot, onion
100 g bacon
2 glasses red wine
3 juniper berries

1 clove
3 sprigs rosemary
Fine salt, to taste
7 tbsp extra virgin olive oil
600 g mashed potatoes*

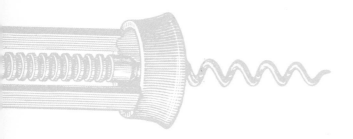

METHOD

Cut the meat into small pieces.
Peel, wash and cut the vegetables into small cubes.
Put 5 tablespoons of oil in a saucepan with the meat. Season with salt.
Cook on a high heat with the lid until it is well browned.
After browning, pour a glass of red wine and let it evaporate.
At this point, remove part of the cooking liquid, which also contains the fat, and add the vegetables, spices and two tablespoons of oil.
Sauté and reduce again with the wine.
Add three glasses of water, cover, reduce the heat and simmer for at least an hour.
Cut the bacon finely and sauté gently.
Finally, season the stew with the fried bacon and serve in a hot dish accompanied with mashed potatoes.

EGG AND CREAM WITH STEWED CABBAGE, APPLE AND PIAVE CHEESE

SERVES **4**

4 eggs
250 ml cream
300 g cabbage
60 g butter
100 g boiled beetroot
50 g onion

1 bay leaf
100 g mature Piave cheese
1 green apple
Salt, to taste
Black pepper, to taste

METHOD

Cut the cabbage into thin strips and put to cook in a saucepan over a low heat with the butter and bay leaf, cover with the lid.
Cut the beets into small cubes and julienne the onion.
Add to the cabbage and cook for 10 minutes. Add the salt towards the end of the cooking time.
Meanwhile, grease some casseroles and place in each the raw egg.
Put the cream in a bowl and season with salt and pepper.
Cover the egg with the cream.
Put some water in a baking dish and place the casseroles inside.
Bake at 160° C for 10 minutes.
Serve the casseroles hot, topped with cheese shavings, accompanied with cabbage and slices of green apple cut into julienne strips.

CHICKEN WITH PEPPERS

SERVES **4**

4 chicken thighs
3 sprigs rosemary
2 peppers
½ cup vinegar
1 onion

1 **tbsp** sugar
3 **sprigs** mint
200 g tomato puree
2 **tbsp** extra virgin olive oil
Fine salt, to taste

METHOD

Wash the peppers, cut them in half, remove the seeds and pulp, then cut into diamond shapes.

Boil the peppers in boiling water and vinegar for 3 minutes.

Julienne the onion and place it in a casserole with 2 tablespoons of olive oil.

Wilt the onions and add the blanched peppers, the salt and the sugar.

When the sugar begins to caramelise, add 2 tablespoons of vinegar and let it evaporate.

Add the tomato puree and cook on low heat for 30 minutes.

Finally add the mint leaves.

Clean the chicken, remove the feathers, toss it on the flame and wash.

In a greased baking dish place the chicken with the skin side up.

Rub the meat with salt and rosemary.

Bake at 80°C for 2 hours.

After the required time, remove the fat that has melted and bake at 180°C for 15 minutes.

Sprinkle with the pepper sauce and bake again at 160°C for 15 minutes for it to flavour well.

TURKEY DUMPLINGS FILLED WITH MORTADELLA AND MYRTLE AND SWEET AND SOUR ONIONS

SERVES **4**

4 slices mortadella
4 slices turkey
100 g celery
100 g carrots
3 sprigs myrtle
3 sage leaves
3 sprigs rosemary

3 tbsp extra virgin olive oil
300 g baby onions
60 g butter
1 tbsp sugar
2 tbsp white wine vinegar
Fine salt, to taste

METHOD

Wash and clean the onions.

Take a pan and sprinkle the bottom with sugar, butter and a pinch of salt.

Add the onions and let them caramelise on the sugar, without turning.

Once this is browned, pour the vinegar, cover and continue cooking over a low heat until the onions are cooked.

Wash and clean the carrots and celery. Cut them into sticks.

Separately, beat the turkey slices with a lightly moistened meat mallet, put the celery and carrots on top.

Open the slices of mortadella on the table.

Arrange on each slice of mortadella a slice of turkey with the vegetables.

Close into a dumpling and tie with string as you would with a roast.

At the bottom of a pot, lay the herbs and pour half a glass of water and oil.

Add the turkey dumplings and steam them.

Cook on a high heat until the water begins to boil, then reduce to a minimum and keeping the lid on, continue cooking.

Serve the dumplings with the caramelised onions.

ROAST PORK WITH GRAPPA AND BLUEBERRY JAM

SERVES **6**

1.2 **kg** fresh pork bacon
2 sprigs rosemary
100 **g** carrots
100 **g** celery
200 **g** onions
2 glasses white wine

½ glass grappa,
1 **tbsp** honey
400 **g** mashed potato*
4 **tsps** blueberry jam
Fine salt, to taste

METHOD

Take the bacon and make some cuts on the outer rind.

Put it in a saucepan with 1 glass of wine and cover with the lid. Cook on a low heat.

After 15 minutes, add the chopped vegetables, rosemary and honey.

Sauté and pour the remaining wine and grappa. Once evaporated, add 1 litre of water, cover and cook for 4 hours on a low heat.

Once the roast is ready, let it rest for fifteen minutes before slicing it.

Slice and serve with the gravy, mashed potatoes and a teaspoon of blueberry jam.

ITALIAN-STYLE LAMB WITH ENGLISH PUDDINGS

SERVES **4**

500 g lamb leg
3 sprigs rosemary
2 sage leaves
2 cloves garlic
1 glass white wine
1 glass water
100 g peeled tomatoes

4 tbsp extra virgin olive oil
Fine salt, to taste
FOR THE CUPCAKES
4 eggs
200 g "00" flour
400 ml milk
Fine salt, to taste

METHOD

Combine in a bowl the eggs, salt, milk and stir. Add the flour and mix well.
Leave it to rest for two hours.
Put the mixture into moulds and bake in oven at 250°C.
Meanwhile, cut the meat into cubes and season with salt and oil.
Sauté in a hot non-stick pan, taking care not to turn it. Cover with the lid and continue cooking.
In the meantime, chop the sage, garlic and rosemary.
Add the chopped herbs to the meat.
When the meat is browned, pour in the white wine and let it evaporate.
Add the peeled tomatoes and a glass of water.
Cook for another 7-8 minutes, until the sauce has thickened.
Serve the lamb with the puddings.

CHICKEN PATTIES IN RED SWEET AND SOUR SAUCE

SERVES **4**

200 g chicken breast
150 g white bread, without crust
2g pink pepper
2 egg whites
Fine salt, to taste

**FOR THE SWEET
AND SOUR SAUCE**
300 g red bell peppers

100 g fresh onion
5 capers
50 g pitted green olives
2 sprigs parsley
4 tbsp extra virgin olive oil
1 tbsp sugar
2 g salt
50 g vinegar

METHOD

For the patties: Combine the ingredients in a bowl (they must be very cold), mix them and then pass them in a blender or in a meat grinder, until they become a smooth paste. Let the mixture rest for at least 30 minutes in the refrigerator. Shape into patties weighing about 40 g each.
Cook the patties in a pan with a little oil.
For the sauce: Peel and wash the vegetables.
Sauté the chopped onion in the oil over a gentle heat.
Add the diced peppers, olives and capers, finely chopped, and finally the chopped parsley.
Add the salt and sugar and cook with the lid.
When the vegetables begin to caramelise, add the vinegar to the sauce and let it evaporate.
Serve the patties accompanied with the sweet and sour sauce.

AUBERGINES STUFFED WITH SQUID

SERVES **4**

4 squid
1 clove garlic
½ glass white wine
2 aubergines
½ l Béchamel*

2 dried tomatoes
2 sprigs parsley
2 eggs
4 **tbsp** extra virgin olive oil
Fine salt, to taste

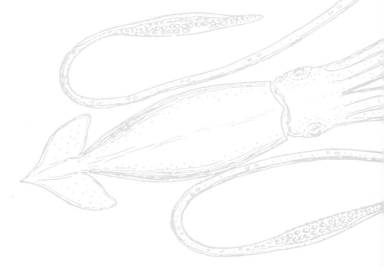

METHOD

Clean and wash the squid, cut into strips.
Put the oil in a pan, add the squid, garlic and simmer with the lid on.
Wash the aubergines and cut them in half, empty them and put the pulp obtained to cook with the squid. Set aside the emptied aubergine skins.
Sauté well, pour in the white wine and let it evaporate.
Once ready, blend the mixture in a food processor. Pour it in a bowl and let it cool.
Add the béchamel, eggs, dried tomatoes and parsley, stir well.
Stuff the aubergines with the mixture.
Bake at 180° C for 25 minutes.
Let it rest before serving.

BOILED MEAT WITH ONION SAUCE

SERVES **4**

400 g boiled beef* (also shin or other boiled meat)
300 g carrots boiled with salt and sugar
3 medium potatoes, boiled
6 cherry tomatoes
3 sprigs parsley
2 sprigs marjoram
2 tbsp extra virgin olive oil

FOR THE ONION SAUCE
200 g blanched red onions
60 g ginger
2 tbsp sugar
½ tbsp chilli
2 tbsp extra virgin olive oil
2 tbsp apple cider vinegar

METHOD

Cut the boiled meat into cubes and cook in a pan with oil, without turning.
Cut the tomatoes into quarters and add to the boiled meat along with the marjoram and parsley.
For the sauce, peel the ginger and cut it into small pieces, add it to the onion cut into julienne strips.
Put them in a saucepan and add the chilli, salt, sugar and oil.
Cook over moderate heat with the lid and towards the end of the cooking time add the vinegar.
Let it evaporate and set aside.
Cut the potatoes and carrots into cubes and place them on the bottom of the plate.
Place the boiled meat over it with the onion sauce on the side.

BRAISED PORK
WITH FENNEL AND PROSECCO

SERVES **4**

1 **kg** pork shoulder
750 **ml** Prosecco
750 **ml** water
120 **g** salt
2 leeks
1 fennel bulbs
2 red bell peppers

2 Roman courgettes
1 aubergine
2 peeled potatoes
1 red onion
3 sprigs rosemary
4 **tbsp** extra virgin olive oil

METHOD

Peel and wash the fennel and leek. Cut them into chunks.
Put the pork shoulder in a deep pan with the fennel, leeks, salt, water and wine.
Cook with the lid on a low heat for about 4 hours.
Once the water has dried up, turn up the heat and brown the meat without covering it.
Wash and clean peppers, courgettes, aubergine, onions and potatoes.
Cut all into strips.
Season the vegetables with salt, olive oil and rosemary and place on a baking sheet, cover with aluminium foil.
Bake at 120° C for 10 minutes, remove the aluminium and increase the temperature to 150° C until the end of the cooking.
Let the meat rest before cutting it and serve with vegetables.

PORK SLICES WITH BEANS AND POTATOES

SERVES **4**

600 g pork (leg or loin)
200 g cooked beans
400 g purple potatoes, boiled
2 g chives
150 g fresh tomato

200 g cooked chard
1 glass blonde beer
6 tbsp extra virgin olive oil
"OO" flour, as needed
Fine salt, to taste

METHOD

Peel and slice the potatoes.
Cook in a pan with 2 tablespoons of olive oil, salt and chopped chives. Keep to one side.
Cut the pork strips, salt and lightly flour them.
Put the oil in a pan and when it is hot, cook the slices of pork in it, taking care not to turn them straight away. When it is almost cooked, add the beans and stir.
Separately, prepare the salad by cutting the chard into pieces, add the tomato cut into cubes, season with salt.
Sauté the chard in the pan with a glass of beer. Continue to cook until evaporated.
Prepare the dish by placing the potatoes on the bottom, the pork and beans on top and finally the chard.

STEWED TUNA WITH TOMATO AND BASIL SAUCE

SERVES **4**

4 thin slices of fresh tuna
2 g oregano
4 slices cheek bacon
400 g cherry tomatoes
8 basil leaves
8 slices homemade bread

1 clove garlic
120 g celery hearts
4 tbsp extra virgin olive oil
Fine salt, to taste
Black pepper, to taste

METHOD

Wash and peel the celery and cut it into cubes of 2 mm per side. Keep to one side.
Cut the bread into slices, rub the garlic and toast on the griddle.
In a pan, grill the slices of cheek lard.
Meanwhile, salt and pepper on both sides the tuna steaks, adding oregano.
It is important that the oregano is left to rehydrate a bit on the moist tuna so that it does not burn whilst cooking.
Remove the cheek lard from the pan and place the tuna over the melted fat.
Turn the slices only when they start to "sweat".
Centrifuge the tomatoes, season the juice obtained with salt and basil.
Heat the tomato sauce in a pan.
Put the tomato sauce in a bowl, put the tuna on top, then the slices of cheek lard and sprinkle with diced celery, accompanied with garlic croutons.

FRIED CHICKEN BREAST
IN GREEN BATTER WITH SALAD

SERVES **4**

4 slices chicken breast
FOR THE BATTER
80 g flour
80 g Pecorino cheese, grated
12 capers
3 sprigs parsley
70 g pine nuts
6 basil leaves

2 tbsp extra virgin olive oil
Baking soda, 1 pinch
Peanut oil for frying
TO ACCOMPANY
200 g cut salad
1 lemon
2 tbsp extra virgin olive oil

METHOD

Prepare the batter by whisking in a blender the basil, capers, parsley, pine nuts, pecorino cheese and a dash of water.

The ingredients should be very cold, to limit oxidation.

Transfer the mixture into a bowl and add the flour, salt, baking soda, olive oil and mix well.

Dip the slices of chicken cut into strips in the batter and proceed with frying in deep hot oil.

Serve the chicken sticks hot accompanied by fresh salad dressed with olive oil and lemon.

STRIPS OF BEEF WITH RICE PILAF AND JULIENNE VEGETABLES

SERVES **4**

150 g wild rice
½ onion
6 cloves
2 l vegetable stock*
500 g thin slices of beef

200 g peppers
200 g tomatoes
200 g white cabbage
1 clove garlic
Fine salt to taste
Extra virgin olive oil to taste

METHOD

Cut the onion in half and stick the cloves into the outer part of the onion.
Roast the onion in a small saucepan (without the addition of water or fat) until it is light brown.
Put two tablespoons of oil, the rice and roasted onion into a saucepan and cover with the boiling stock.
Cover and cook on a medium heat.
Season the slices of meat with salt and oil.
Julienne (cut into thin strips) the peppers, tomatoes and cabbage.
Rub a bowl with the garlic, put the chopped vegetables into the bowl and season with salt and oil.
Put three tablespoons of olive oil into a frying pan on a high heat and quickly sear the meat, tearing it into pieces using a spatula and a knife.
Remove the meat and sear the vegetables in the same pan.
Serve the meat on a plate accompanied by the rice and vegetables.

WHITE POLENTA CAKE WITH SEARED RADICCHIO AND SCHIZ CHEESE

INGREDIENTS FOR **ONE** CAKE

250 g white corn flour
2 heads radicchio
150 g Schiz cheese
½ cup cream
Fine salt to taste

Black pepper to taste
1 cup cooked grape must (or ready balsamic glaze)
Extra virgin olive oil to taste

METHOD

Bring 1 litre of water to the boil in a deep saucepan, add salt and pour in the corn flour, stirring with a whisk to avoid lumps.
Continue cooking on low heat, stirring occasionally for 40 minutes.
In the mean time, prepare the radicchio, clean, cut into four, wash and drain.
Season the radicchio with salt and oil, arrange on a baking sheet and bake at 200° C for 10 minutes, lower the temperature and leave it to wilt a little.
Cut Schiz cheese into slices, wetting the blade of the knife so the cheese doesn't stick to it.
Line a greased round baking tin with the radicchio, arranging it in a radial pattern, cover with slices of cheese, the cream and finally the polenta. Garnish with the must and bake at 110° C for 1 hour.
Serve with good salami.

RED POTATO SALAD WITH MOZZARELLA, BACON AND LETTUCE

SERVES **4**

400 g red potatoes
10 g chives
1 head lettuce, washed
100 g bacon

½ glass white wine
2 hard boiled egg yolks
180 g mozzarella
Fine salt to taste

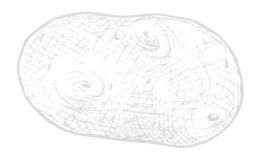

METHOD

Cut the bacon into thin strips, put it into a bowl and marinate in the white wine for about an hour.

Put the bacon in a frying pan without oil, cover and fry over a low heat.

Wash the potatoes, preferably of the same size, put them into a saucepan with cold water and salt, bring to the boil and cook.

Once cooked, leave them to cool completely and peel.

Cut the lettuce into thin strips (julienne), dice the potatoes and chop the chives.

Put everything in a bowl and season with the bacon fat.

Prepare the dish by placing the potato salad at the bottom, place the mozzarella on top of the salad and finally add the crispy bacon with the sieved hard-boiled egg yolk.

DESSERT

"S" BISCUITS WITH SAFFRON AND RED WINE

INGREDIENTS

600 g "00" flour
4 whole eggs
350 g soft butter
250 g sugar

1 g saffron
½ l red wine
8 g baking powder

METHOD

First, put the wine in a saucepan and let it reduce over a low heat, until it has an oily consistency.

When it is ready, leave it to cool down and start making the flavoured sugars.

To make saffron sugar just dissolve the saffron in a little water and add 125g of sugar; for the wine sugar, add to the remaining 125g of sugar the wine reduction and mix well. Keep to one side.

Combine the flour and baking powder in a bowl. In another bowl, beat the softened butter with the eggs.

Pour the dry ingredients into the wet ones and mix well until you get a homogeneous mixture.

To obtain a crumbly short crust pastry, you need to be careful not to work the dough for too long.

Divide the dough into two equal parts, add one flavoured sugar to each half of dough, always working the dough quickly.

Place the different coloured dough on top of each other, cut into strips, shape into cylinders and cut them into biscuits. Arrange the biscuits on a baking sheet covered with parchment paper, sprinkle the surface with sugar and bake in the oven at 150° C for 15-20 minutes.

CHOCOLIVE POT PIE

SERVES **4**

300 g short crust pastry*
300 g pastry cream*
200 ml milk
250 g dark chocolate
4 egg yolks

15 g corn starch
3 tbsp extra virgin olive oil
200 g strawberry ice cream
4 moulds

METHOD

Bring the milk to the boil in a saucepan.

Meanwhile, coarsely chop the chocolate. When the milk is hot, remove it from the heat, add the chopped chocolate and stir until completely dissolved.

Separately, mix the egg yolks with the starch and oil in a bowl, use a whisk (to avoid lumps) and mix slowly (the mixture should not be beaten).

Stir in the chocolate mixture and continue to mix well.

Let the mixture cool completely.

Grease and flour the moulds.

Roll out the very cold pastry to half a centimetre thick, cut out discs, prick lightly with a fork and line the moulds with the pastry, making it adhere well to them.

Use a piping bag to pipe a ring of pastry cream inside the pastry, fill the hole in the middle with the cold chocolate cream.

Cover the tartlets with another disc of pastry and brush with the beaten egg yolk.

Bake in a preheated oven at 150° C for about 20 minutes.

Leave to cool and remove from the moulds.

Serve the pies accompanied by a scoop of strawberry ice cream.

HAZELNUT, APPLE AND JAM SLICES

SERVES **4**

250 g chopped hazelnuts
200 g demerara sugar
80 g "00" flour

3 egg whites
150 g blueberry jam
50 g apples (golden or rennet)

METHOD

Combine the chopped hazelnuts, demerara sugar and flour in a bowl.
Mix these dry ingredients well, then add the egg whites.
Knead the mixture well with your hands until it is homogeneous and compact.
Cover the dough with plastic wrap and leave it to rest in the refrigerator for at least 10-12 hours.
After this time, butter and flour a loaf tin.
Place a layer of the hazelnut mixture (half of the dough) on the bottom of the tin.
Wash and clean the apples, cut them into thick slices, place them in the tin, completely covering the hazelnut layer.
Cover the apples with a few spoonfuls of blueberry jam and finish with a final layer of hazelnut mixture.
Bake in a preheated oven at 120° C degrees for 15 -20 minutes, then reduce the heat to 90° C and continue baking for 1 hour.
When the cake has cooled, cut it into slices and serve.

APPLE PIE

INGREDIENTS FOR **1** PIE

100 g "00" flour
100 g ground almonds
180 g sugar
6 whole eggs
30 g butter

150 g berries
3 apples (rennet)
40 g demerara sugar
1 tsp powdered gelatine

METHOD

Prepare the gelatine by dissolving it in water in a saucepan.
When the gelatine starts boiling, add the berries, turn off the heat and leave to cool.
Grease a cake tin well then dust it with cane sugar.
Put the loaf tin on a low heat and let the sugar caramelise.
Meanwhile, peel the apples and cut them into thick slices. Use cold apples if possible as they oxidise more slowly.
When the caramel is golden, place the apple wedges in the tin in a radial pattern.
Separately, beat the eggs and sugar (in a blender) until the mixture is light and fluffy.
Then stir in the sifted flour a little at a time, being careful not to remove the air from the mixture, stir with a spoon from the bottom to the top.
Remove the tin with the apples from the heat, pour over the mixture and bake the pie at 180° C for 15 minutes, then reduce the heat to 140° C and cook for another 20 minutes.
When the pie has cooled, spread the berry gelatine on the top using a spatula.

SEMOLINA CAKE WITH APRICOTS IN SYRUP

INGREDIENTS FOR **1** CAKE

300 g short crust pastry*
500 ml milk
60 g semolina
3 egg yolks

70 g sugar
Apricots in syrup, to taste
1 lemon zest and juice
Pinch of fine salt

METHOD

Put the milk with a pinch of salt in a saucepan to heat.
In a bowl beat the egg yolks with the sugar, flavouring everything with lemon zest and a little juice.
Work the mixture well until it becomes light and fluffy.
Finally add the semolina and let it rest.
As soon as the milk has started to boil, pour it a little at a time, in the egg mixture, stirring with a whisk.
Put the mixture in the pan and cook on a low heat, until the semolina is cooked and the cream has reached the right consistency.
Grease and flour a cake pan and line with the pastry spread to a thickness of ½ centimetre.
Pour a ½ cm layer of semolina cream.
Arrange the apricots (cut in half) in a radial pattern on the semolina cream.
Cover with the remaining cream and bake at 150° C for at least 30 minutes.
Remove from the oven, let it rest and serve warm with fresh whipped cream.

NOUGAT AND RICOTTA BOMB

INGREDIENTS FOR **1** PIE

200 g discs of sponge cake
(without crust) *
250 g white almond nougat
(Torrone abruzzese)
250 g sheep milk ricotta,
300 g dark chocolate

FOR THE SYRUP
100 g sugar
100 g water
½ glass Italian gentian liqueur
1 sachet saffron

METHOD

Reduce the nougat into pieces and chop rather finely in a blender.
Sift the ricotta, collecting it in a bowl along with the nougat.
Stir the mixture well and store in the refrigerator for at least 30 minutes.
In the meantime, prepare the syrup: combine in a saucepan the sugar, saffron,
water and liqueur. Put it all on the heat and as soon as it starts to boil, let it cool.
With the cold liquid moisten well the sponge cake and use it to line a
hemispherical mould. Fill the mould with the ricotta mixture, alternating with
layers of wet sponge, until you close the mould with it.
Let it stand in the refrigerator for at least 8-10 hours.
After this time, reverse the "bomb" on a baking tray.
Melt the chocolate in the microwave or bain-marie, then pour it on the cake well
cold (possibly after tempered), so as to form a uniform layer that covers the
whole. Let the chocolate harden before cutting into slices and serve.

AUBERGINE AND CHOCOLATE DESSERT

SERVES **4**

300 g discs of sponge cake
(without crust)*
1 aubergine
½ l milk
4 egg yolks
120 g sugar
35 g corn starch

150 g dark chocolate
150 g sweetened ricotta
Candied fruit to decorate

FOR THE SYRUP
1 glass Marsala
1 glass milk

METHOD

Wash the aubergine and make a few deep cuts on the surface.
Cook it on an oven grill at 250° C for about 20 minutes.
Once cooked, transfer it into a container and close it tightly with plastic wrap,
then let it cool: this way it will be easier to remove the bitter and tough peel.
After removing the aubergine pulp, blend it and keep the puree to one side.
Meanwhile, chop the chocolate and boil the milk.
Beat the egg yolks in a bowl with the sugar and starch; dilute with half of the hot milk
in the bowl and then pour it back into the saucepan with the rest of the hot milk.
Keep it all on a medium heat, stirring, and when the cream starts to thicken, add
the chopped aubergine and simmer for 5 minutes.
As the last step, add the chocolate to the cream, stirring until completely dissolved.
Prepare the syrup for the cake by mixing equal parts of milk and marsala.
Moisten the discs of sponge cake evenly with the syrup.
Make the cake by wetting 3 discs and alternating with the chocolate and
aubergine cream. Cover with the sweetened ricotta cheese and decorate with
candied fruit.

CORN KISSES

INGREDIENTS

150 g "00" flour
125 g yellow corn flour
40 g raisins
125 g butter
75 g sugar
4 egg yolks

8 g baking powder
1 tbsp aniseed
200 g white chocolate
100 g chopped pistachios
Grated rind of one lemon
Grappa, to taste

METHOD

First of all, put the raisins in the grappa to rehydrate for at least two hours.
After this time, squeeze the raisins and keep them aside.
Melt the butter in a saucepan and let it cool.
Mix the egg yolks in a bowl with the butter, starch and lemon zest.
Add the white flour and corn flour to the mixture, kneading for the minimum time necessary to make the mixture homogeneous. Finally, add the raisins to the mixture.
Let the dough rest for at least 8 hours.
After this time, re-work the dough and add a pinch of yeast.
Make small balls with the mixture, place them on a baking sheet lined with parchment paper and cook in a preheated oven at 130° C for 40 minutes.
Once cool, take two biscuits at a time and put in the middle some melted white chocolate and chopped pistachios.

POT PIE WITH CREAM OF CARROTS AND ALMONDS

SERVES **6**

300 g short crust pastry*
½ l almond milk
4 egg yolks
50 g corn starch

100 g sugar
250 g boiled carrots
60 g coloured sugar strands
1 beaten egg

METHOD

This recipe is suitable for people who are intolerant to lactose and milk in general.
Puree the carrots that have previously been boiled (water, sugar, a pinch of salt).
Place the carrot puree in a saucepan with the almond milk, and cook over a low heat.
Meanwhile, beat the egg yolks in a bowl with the sugar and starch.
Once the mixture with almonds and carrots has started to boil, pour it on the
egg mixture, stirring.
Put the pan back on the heat, leaving the cream to thicken for a few minutes.
Once it is ready, let it cool.
Grease and flour some moulds and line the inside with discs of pastry spread to
a thickness of ½ centimetre, so that it adheres well to the sides if the moulds.
Fill the moulds with the cream and close with another disk of pastry. Brush the
surface with beaten egg and sprinkle with the sugar strands.
Bake in a preheated oven at 145-150° C for about 30 minutes.

HAZELNUT CREAM ON CRISPY WAFFLES

SERVES **4**

FOR THE WAFFLES
250 g "00" flour
2 whole eggs
150 g butter
170 g sugar
1 glass milk
Flavourings (vanilla and ½ grated lemon)

FOR THE HAZELNUT CREAM
250 ml whole milk
125 g dark chocolate
125 g milk chocolate
30 g corn starch
150 g roasted hazelnuts

METHOD

Coarsely chop the dark chocolate.
Whisk the milk and hazelnuts in a food processor.
Transfer everything into a saucepan and add the starch, using a whisk to avoid lumps.
Put the saucepan over a low heat, stirring and start adding the chocolate.
Once it has completely melted, remove the pan from the heat and let it cool.
Prepare the pastry for the waffles now, beating eggs with the butter, sugar, milk and flavourings.
Finally add at once the flour, and taking care not to knead it too much, put the dough in the refrigerator, so as to let the butter slightly thicken: this way the batter will be more dense and stable in cooking.
Cook the waffles in the specific machine.
Then just spread the hazelnut cream on the waffles and top with whipped cream.

BI-FLAVOURED ALMOND MOUSSE

SERVES **8**

250 g peeled almonds
100 g sugar
1 bitter almond
½ l almond milk
15 g gelatine sheets

300 ml whipped cream
150 g shortbread biscuits
300 g cherries
1 small glass grappa

METHOD

Put the almond milk, almonds, sugar and bitter almond in a blender.
Blend all the ingredients until the mixture is smooth and homogeneous. Let it rest in refrigerator.
Strain the mixture obtained with the chinois, to remove impurities.
Rehydrate the gelatine in cold water for 6-7 minutes, squeeze and heat it in the microwave with a little water. Then add it to the mixture, stirring well with a whisk.
Continue incorporating the whipped cream into the mixture (do not worry if it deflates a little), to obtain a mousse.
With the help of a pastry bag, fill some bowls with the mousse and store them in a refrigerator to cool.
Before serving, prepare the cherries by pitting them and wetting them with a little grappa and tossing them in the pan for a few minutes.
Remove the bowls from the refrigerator and place the hot cherries and hot biscuits on the very cold mousse.
Serve the dessert with a glass of Muscat wine.

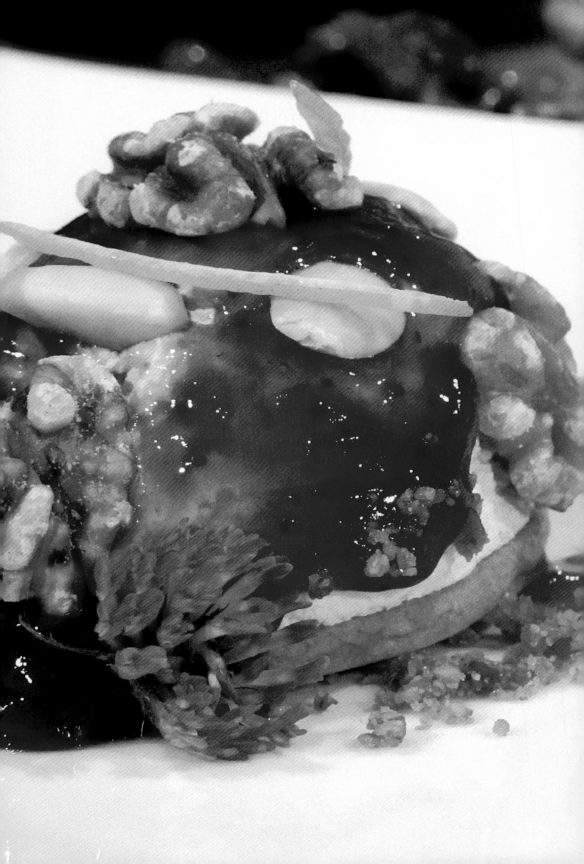

ST. MICHAEL'S CUP CAKE

INGREDIENTS FOR **10** CUP CAKES

100 g short crust pastry*
12 g gelatine sheets
½ l fresh cream
50 g almonds
50 g chopped walnuts
200 g chopped almond brittle
Strawberry jam

FOR THE PÂTE À BOMBE
5 yolks (100 g)
200 g sugar
100 g water

METHOD

Begin to make the pâte à bombe by putting the egg yolks in a blender, and mixing at medium speed.

Boil the water and sugar in a saucepan until you get a syrup at a temperature of about 118° C. Once the temperature is reached, remove the pan from the heat and pour the syrup onto the egg yolks in the blender, continuing to mix and increasing the speed.

Continue beating the mixture until it is fluffy and almost cold.

Rehydrate the gelatine in cold water for 6-7 minutes, squeeze and heat it in the microwave with a little water. Then add it to the pâte à bombe, stirring well with a whisk.

Finally add the whipped cream, chopped nuts and chopped brittle.

Pour the mixture into small silicone moulds, and put them in the freezer, making sure to cover them with plastic wrap.

Before serving, transfer for 10-15 minutes to the refrigerator.

To finish, roll out the short crust pastry to a thickness of ½ centimetre and cut into little discs. Pierce them with a fork and bake them on a baking sheet lined with parchment paper at 145° C for about 10-15 minutes.

These will form the basis of the parfaits, to be placed under each portion when it is ready to be served.

Accompany it all with a spoonful of strawberry jam and walnuts.

SAVARIN WITH CHESTNUT FLOUR

SERVES **4**

200 g chestnut flour
150 g chestnut puree
200 g hazelnut flour
120 g sugar
120 g butter
1 pinch cinnamon

8 g baking powder
1 glass milk
2 whole eggs
2 apples
Apricot jam

METHOD

Wash, peel and dice the apples.
Melt the apricot jam in a pan over a low heat, add the diced apples and cook for a few minutes. Keep to one side.
Mix in a bowl the chestnut flour, the hazelnut flour, the baking powder and the sugar.
In another bowl, mix together using with a whisk the eggs, milk, warm melted butter, the chestnut puree and the cinnamon.
Add the dry ingredients to the liquid ones, mixing just enough to obtain a smooth and homogeneous mixture.
Grease and flour the moulds for the savarins.
Half-fill them with the mixture and bake at 150° C for 15-20 minutes.
Before serving, let them stand 1 minute to redistribute the liquid inside.
Serve the savarin with the apples in the centre.

CANESTRELLI MY WAY

INGREDIENTS

450 g "00" flour
100 g ground almonds
150 g icing sugar
300 g soft butter

2 whole eggs
4 g baking powder
1 lemon
Milk, as required

METHOD

In a blender, mix the white flour and the almond flour, then add the yeast, the soft butter and lemon zest until it reaches a sandy texture.

Add to the mixture first the icing sugar, then the beaten eggs (slowly), until the mixture is homogeneous and compact.

The procedure must be done quickly so that the dough is soft and crumbly after baking.

Let the dough rest in the refrigerator for at least 2 hours.

Roll out to a thickness of 1 cm, and cut out little flowers with a biscuit mould.

Arrange the biscuits on a baking sheet lined with parchment paper, brush them with a little milk and bake at 140° - 150° C for 20 minutes.

When they are ready, let them cool and sprinkle with plenty of icing sugar.

ITALIAN CANTUCCI

INGREDIENTS

500 g "00" flour
500 g sugar
500 g hazelnuts or almonds
5 whole eggs

16 g baking powder
Black pepper, 10 ground
4 g salt

METHOD

Mix the eggs with the sugar in a bowl using a whisk.

Add the sifted flour with the baking powder, salt, ground pepper and hazelnuts/almonds, blending it all quickly, until you get a homogeneous mixture.

Line a baking sheet with parchment paper and with the dough make 3 cm wide sticks, placing them on the baking sheet.

Bake in a preheated oven at 150° C for about 25 minutes.

Remove from the oven, and with the help of a knife with a smooth and sharp blade cut the sticks immediately, before they cool, into many slices, ½ cm thick (and you have your cantucci).

Bake again at 130° C for another 10 minutes.

STRAWBERRIES WITH CUSTARD, MARSALA EXTRACT, LAYERS OF CRISP BREAD

SERVES 4

300 g stale bread
250 g custard
500 ml Marsala liqueur
3 egg yolks
30 g caster sugar

80 g corn starch
Icing sugar, as required
100 g fresh whipped cream
300 g strawberries

METHOD

Pour the Marsala liqueur in a saucepan and bring to the boil on a low heat.
Meanwhile, mix the egg yolks in a bowl with the sugar and starch, using a whisk.
Pour in the mixture, a little at a time, the boiling Marsala, stirring with a whisk.
Put the mixture on a low heat and let it thicken until it has a hard consistency.
Let it cool and keep it to one side.
Prepare the bread, cut it into thin slices and sprinkle the slices with icing sugar on both sides.
Bake at 90° C until they become completely dry and crisp.
With the help of two pastry bags, filled respectively with the custard and the Marsala cream, on a plate alternate layers of slices of bread with the two creams.
Finish the dish with fresh strawberries and whipped cream.

CREAMED RICE AND HAZELNUT PUDDING

INGREDIENTS FOR **1** MOULD

FOR THE BASE
250 g rusks (biscottes)
10 g cocoa powder
70 g butter
150 g demerara sugar

FOR THE FILLING
100 g rice flour
400 g milk
100 g sugar
1 vanilla pod
3 egg yolks
Crumbled hazelnuts

METHOD

For the base: Chop the rusks in a kitchen machine with the cocoa powder, sugar and melted butter.
For the filling: Slice open the vanilla pod with a knife.
Put the milk in a saucepan then add the open vanilla pod and scraped out seeds. Bring to the boil.
Mix the sugar in a bowl with the eggs and a drop of milk.
Keep stirring and add the rice flour.
Add a spoonful of boiling milk to the mixture, stir well and gently pour in all the milk.
Put everything back in the pan, return to the heat and stir until the mixture thickens.
To complete the dish: Grease a cake tin.
Pour the rusk mixture in the base.
Press down well, pour in the creamed rice and smooth the top.
Bake at 120° C for the first 30 minutes and at 100° C for another 40 minutes.
Leave to cool.
Remove the cake from the mould and serve sprinkled with chopped hazelnuts.

LUCIANO'S FROSTED TARALLI

INGREDIENTS

300 g flour
2 eggs
50 g sugar

1 small glass Marsala
Pinch of fine salt
2 tbsp extra virgin olive oil

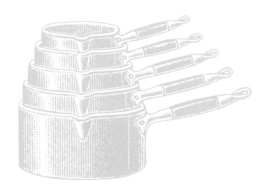

METHOD

Mix all the ingredients, flour, eggs, salt, sugar, oil and Marsala, together on the work surface or in a kitchen machine. Mix to form smooth and elastic dough. Leave the dough to rest for 2-4 hours.

Then roll the dough into long thin cylinders and cut them to the desired length to form doughnuts.

Bring plenty of water to the boil in a saucepan with a pinch of salt, when it boils, drop in a few taralli at a time and take them out with a slotted spoon as soon as they float to the surface.

Drain well and place the taralli on a lightly greased baking sheet, bake at 160° C for 40 minutes.

Meanwhile, prepare the glaze: Put the hot water in a saucepan, dissolve the icing sugar in the ratio 1:1; bring to the boil again, remove from heat and leave to cool. Brush the taralli with the glaze.

DELICIOUS DARK CHOCOLATE AND HAZELNUT CAKE

INGREDIENTS FOR **1** CAKE

500 g "00" flour
150 g demerara sugar
100 ml extra virgin olive oil
½ glass Marsala

8 g baking powder
300 g dark chocolate
300 g fresh Cream
150 g chopped toasted hazelnuts

METHOD

Chop the chocolate coarsely, bring the cream to the boil in a small saucepan, remove from the heat, add the chocolate and stir. Allow to melt, mix well then leave to cool.

Mix together the flour, baking powder and demerara sugar in a bowl.

Gradually add the oil and Marsala, working the mixture with your hands to get crumbs.

Leave the mixture to rest in the refrigerator.

Grease a cake tin, put the crumbs inside, press them down lightly with your hands and cook the cake in a preheated oven at 140° C for about 25 minutes. When cool, place the cake on a wire rack and pour over the melted chocolate and cream, covering it completely.

Sprinkle with chopped toasted hazelnuts and leave in the refrigerator.

Serve cut into large pieces.

BASIC RECIPES

BASIC RECIPES

FISH STOCK

SERVES **4**

3 l water
3 celery stalks
2 carrots
1 brown onion
1 tbsp coarse salt
4 sprigs parsley
Fish bones, heads of cuttlefish, shells
4 black peppercorns

METHOD

Wash and clean the celery, carrot and
onion.
Put the water, the fish and parsley into
a saucepan and start to cook on a low
flame.
When white foam starts to form,
remove it with a skimmer.
Add the vegetables and salt and
continue cooking over a low heat for
about 2 hours.

VEGETABLE STOCK

INGREDIENTS

2 l water
100 g celery
100 g carrots
200 g onions
2 cloves
1 bay leaf
10 g coarse salt

METHOD

Clean the vegetables, cut into pieces,
put into cold water and bring to the
boil. Add the roasted onion and the
bay leaf. Remember to skim the liquid
carefully after it starts boiling again and
keep the fire very low, so that the stock
barely moves.

CHICKEN STOCK

SERVES 4

3 l water
3 celery stalks
2 carrots
1 brown onion
1 tbsp coarse salt
1 bay leaf
1 chicken

METHOD

To clean the chicken, remove the feathers using a pocket knife, singe it and wash well.

Wash and clean the celery, carrot and onion.

Put the water, chicken and bay leaf into a saucepan and start to cook on a low flame.

When white foam starts to form, remove it with a skimmer.

Add the vegetables and salt and continue cooking over a low heat for about 2 hours.

VELVET SAUCE

INGREDIENTS

50 g butter
40 g "00" flour
1 l vegetable broth *

METHOD

Velvet sauces are made primarily with broths, with the adding of a roux (melted butter to which flour is incorporated) in an amount that varies depending on the density you want to achieve.

All broths are good to make a velvet sauce.

Then, melt the butter in a saucepan, add the flour and mix well.

Cook for a few minutes on a low heat. Remove from the heat, add the mixture to the hot broth, stirring with a whisk.

Continue cooking until the broth begins to thicken.

MINESTRONE SOUP

INGREDIENTS

200 g white onions
200 g carrots
100 g celery
200 g courgettes
300 g potatoes
150 g cauliflower
100 g pinto beans
100 g peas
Water, as needed
Extra virgin olive oil to taste
Fine salt, to taste
Grated cheese, to taste

METHOD

Peel and wash the vegetables.
Cut the onion, carrots, celery,
courgettes, diced potatoes.
Make small peaks with the cauliflower.
Put the diced vegetables, peas and
beans in a saucepan.
Cover with water and add salt to taste.
Cook on a medium heat with the lid on
until the vegetables are cooked.
Serve with a drizzle of olive oil and
grated cheese to taste.

TOMATO SAUCE

INGREDIENTS

2 kg peeled tomatoes
15 g basil
100 g onions
30 g extra virgin olive oil
Fine salt to taste

METHOD

Finely chop the onion.
Cook the onion in a saucepan with
the olive oil over a low heat.
Liquidise the tomatoes.
Cook the tomatoes with basil in a
saucepan on a gentle heat.
When the onion is wilted and golden,
add it to the tomatoes.
Cook over a medium heat for one
hour.
Season with salt.

TOMATO SLICES
(FOR TOMATO CONCASSÉ)

To achieve the best result with this operation, we recommend using ripe and refrigerated tomatoes.
Wash the tomatoes, make a cross on the bottom and put them in boiling water, leaving them immersed for fifteen seconds, then cool them quickly by dipping them in water and ice.
Drain them again. Now, remove the skin, which will come away easily. Cut the tomatoes into four, removing even the aqueous interior, including the seeds.
This way you will get tomato slices that are useful for various culinary preparations.
Tomato slices cut into small cubes are called tomato concassé.

SWEET AND SOUR ONION

INGREDIENTS

200 g sliced onion
50 g extra virgin olive oil
2 level tbsp sugar
2 pinches fine salt
8 basil leaves
1 tbsp white wine vinegar
1 tbsp tomato paste

METHOD

Put the olive oil, onion, sugar and salt in a saucepan.
Fry well.
Deglaze with the vinegar.
Add the basil.
Add the tomato paste.
Reduce.

SWEET AND SOUR SAUCE

INGREDIENTS

60 g onion
50 g extra virgin olive oil
250 g red bell peppers
15 g olives
2 level tbsp sugar
2 pinches fine salt
8 basil leaves
100 ml white wine vinegar
1 tin peeled tomatoes

METHOD

Cut the peppers into cubes of 2mm per side, chop the onion.
Cut the olives coarsely.
Put the olive oil, onion, sugar and salt in a saucepan.
Fry well.
Pour the vinegar and let it evaporate.
Add the basil.
Add the tomatoes previously blended.
Let it reduce.

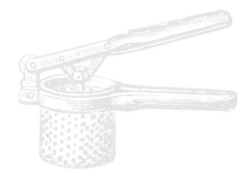

POTATO CHIPS

INGREDIENTS

Potatoes
Oil for frying

METHOD

Wash the potatoes and peel them.
Cut the potatoes into chips using the slicer set at a thickness of 1.5.
Put them for 15 minutes under cold running water.
Drain the potatoes and centrifuge them
Fry them in oil at 190° C for 2 - 2.5 minutes.
Drain on paper towels.
Season with salt.

MASHED POTATOES

INGREDIENTS

1 **kg** floury potatoes
50 **g** butter
300 **ml** milk
Fine salt, to taste
Pinch of nutmeg

METHOD

Wash the potatoes well, place them in a saucepan, cover with cold water and add salt.
Cook on a low heat until the potatoes are cooked.
Drain, and remove the peel while they are still hot. Reduce them to a pulp with a potato masher, put them in a saucepan and add the salt, nutmeg, butter in small pieces and work vigorously with a whisk; finally slowly add the boiling milk.

POTATO GNOCCHI

SERVES **4**

1 **kg** potatoes
300 **g** "00" flour
2 egg yolks
Pinch of fine salt
Pinch of nutmeg

METHOD

Place the potatoes in their skins in cold water, bring to the boil and cook.
Peel and mash as soon as they are cooked and allow them to cool.
When they are cooled completely, place them in a pile, add the egg yolks, salt and nutmeg then begin to knead thoroughly.
When the ingredients are blended very well, add the flour and mix it in the shortest possible time.
Shape the gnocchi by first rolling the dough into a roll 2 cm wide, then cut the gnocchi and place on a floured tray.
If you wish, you can make ridges on the gnocchi by sliding each one on a fork, crushing it slightly.

MUSHROOM FLAVOURED GNOCCHI

SERVES **4**

3 l water
3 celery stalks
2 carrots
1 brown onion
1 tbsp coarse salt
4 sprigs parsley
Fish bones, heads of cuttlefish, shells
4 black peppercorns

METHOD

Clean, wash and chop the mushrooms.
Put the oil and garlic into a frying
pan, add the mushrooms and cook
over a medium heat.
Blend and leave to cool.
Put the cold water into a saucepan,
add the salt and simmer the potatoes
in their skins.
When cooked, peel and mash. Add
the mushrooms.
When cool, stir in the flour, egg yolks,
salt and nutmeg.
Make the dough quickly.
Shape the dough into small beads
(about 1.5 cm in diameter), press
them one by one on the back of a
fork to created ridges and arrange
them on a tray with flour.
Cook them in plenty of salted water,
draining them shortly after they float
to the surface.

POLENTA

INGREDIENTS

500 g corn flour
2 l water
1 tbsp coarse salt

METHOD

Boil the water in a pan. Season with
salt.
Add the corn flour, stirring with a
whisk to avoid lumps.
Continue cooking on a low heat,
stirring occasionally for 40 minutes.

BÉCHAMEL SAUCE

INGREDIENTS

1 l milk
80 g butter
80 g flour
Salt to taste
Pinch of nutmeg

**FOR A VERY THICK BÉCHAMEL
(as required in some recipes):**
500 ml milk
120 g butter
100 g white flour
500 ml milk
120 g butter

METHOD

Heat the milk in a saucepan.
Separately, melt the butter in a small
saucepan, when melted, add the flour
and mix well.
Cook for a few minutes.
Remove from heat, add the flour and
butter mixture (roux) to the milk,
stirring with a whisk.
Then continue to cook gently until
the sauce thickens.
Season with salt and nutmeg and stir
occasionally.

CRÊPES

MAKES ABOUT **20** CRÊPES

500 ml milk
200 g "00" flour
4 eggs
Pinch of fine salt
20 ml extra virgin olive oil

METHOD

Put the eggs, salt and flour into a
bowl and stir.
Add the milk a little at a time to
obtain a creamy fairly loose batter.
Pass the batter through a sieve.
Lightly grease a cast iron frying pan
and put it on the heat, when it is hot,
pour a ladle of the mixture into the
pan and spread out quickly. When
it starts to come away from the pan,
turn it and cook the other side; when
it is just cooked remove from the
heat and leave it on the work surface
to cool.

FRITTATA

INGREDIENTS FOR **1** FRITTATA

4 eggs
Fine salt to taste
2 **tbsp** extra virgin olive oil

METHOD

Break the eggs into a bowl, add the
salt and beat.
Heat the frying pan and cover the
bottom with 1 \ 2 tablespoon of oil.
When it is hot, pour half of the eggs
into the pan and stir constantly until
they set.
Pour the scrambled eggs into the raw
eggs, mix well.
Wipe the pan with paper and cover
evenly with the remaining oil.
Do not let the oil get hot enough to
start smoking.
Heat the pan and put in the mixture
of raw and scrambled eggs.
Cover and cook for 2 minutes over a
medium heat.
Remove from heat and leave the
frittata covered (cooking continues)
for another 3 \ 5 minutes.
Turn the frittata over and cook it for
the last time on a high heat for one
minute to brown it.

BASIC RISOTTO

INGREDIENTS FOR **4** PEOPLE

240 g superfine rice
10 g butter
1 litre vegetable stock
200 ml dry white wine

**"MATURATA" ONION
(already cooked in
oil or butter and wine)**
½ onion
20 g butter
½ glass white wine

TO COMPLETE
50 g butter
40 g Parmesan cheese

METHOD

Chop the onion finely and sauté
with butter and white wine until
it becomes almost transparent
("maturata" onion).
Put the butter in a saucepan, add
the rice and cook until it becomes
translucent (toast).
Add the "maturata" onion and cover
with ¾ of the wine, let the wine
evaporate.
Cook over a medium heat, adding the
vegetable stock from time to time.
When cooked, remove from heat
and begin to mix the rice adding the
cold butter cut into small cubes and
finally the grated Parmesan cheese,
incorporating the ingredients well.

EGG PASTA

SERVES **4**

125 g "00" flour
125 g semolina flour
1 egg
175 g water
2 g fine salt

METHOD

Put the flour, semolina, egg, salt and water into the kitchen machine. Mix with the hook until it forms smooth, uniform and homogeneous dough. Leave the dough to rest in the refrigerator for at least 2 hours covered with plastic wrap.
Roll out the dough thinly. Cut depending on usage.

EGG PASTA WITH HONEY

INGREDIENTS

500 g "00" flour
5 egg yolks
1 whole egg
50 g honey
100 g whole milk
3 g fine salt

METHOD

Put the ingredients in the mixer with the hook and knead well to make the dough smooth, firm and homogeneous. Alternatively, knead by hand working the dough vigorously. Leave it to rest in the refrigerator for at least 2 hours covered with plastic wrap.
Use the pasta machine to make tagliolini and leave them to dry on a tray, making sure to flour them lightly.

PIZZA DOUGH

INGREDIENTS

0.5 l whole milk
25 0ml water
8 g sugar
5 g dry yeast
500 g "00" flour
500 g plain flour
9 g fine salt
25 g extra-virgin olive oil
Myrtle, rosemary, fennel

METHOD

Put the water, milk, sugar and yeast into the kitchen machine.
Dissolve and stir for a minute.
Add both types of flour. Mix. Add the salt. Knead for 20 minutes.
Finally add the oil. Knead until it is all incorporated.
Leave to stand at room temperature for 40 minutes.
Leave the dough to rise for 24 hours in the refrigerator at four degrees.
Break the dough and form loaves of 450 g. Put the oil and the dough on a baking sheet. Spread it with your hands and flatten it. Mark it with your fingers.
Leave it to prove for at least 1 hour.
Season with extra virgin olive oil, chopped rosemary and fleur de sel.
Preheat the oven to 220° C with 30% humidity.
Bake at 170° C with 30% humidity for 8 minutes.
Then bake at 175° C with dry heat for 30 minutes.

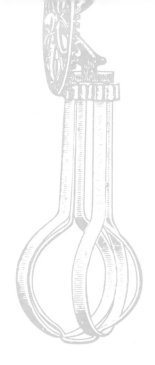

FLOUR AND WATER BATTER

INGREDIENTS

100 g "00" flour
100 g corn starch
170 g cold sparkling water
Fine salt to taste

METHOD

Combine the flour, cornstarch and salt in a bowl. Stir and add the water.
Work the mixture well.
It must be quite thick: the batter must stick to the surface of the spoon when you hold it up.
Cover and leave to rest in the refrigerator for 30 minutes.

MEATBALLS

INGREDIENTS

300 g veal
300 g pork
125 g bread loaf without crust
½ level tbsp oregano
3 sprigs parsley
50 ml milk
2 eggs
¼ grated lemon
1 tsp salt
Peanut oil for frying

METHOD

Combine in a bowl: veal and pork,
cut into pieces, oregano, parsley, egg,
lemon, salt.
In another bowl, combine the bread
cut into pieces with the milk and let
it soften.
Combine the two mixtures and mince
it all twice in the meat grinder.
Make the meatballs.
They should be round and slightly
flattened in the middle.
Fry in deep oil.

BOILED MEAT

INGREDIENTS

1 kg rump, hen, etc.
200 g celery
200 g carrots
200 g onions
5 g parsley
2 l water
10 g coarse salt

METHOD

Prepare a base of mixed vegetables
and herbs in a saucepan, add plenty
of water and cook (cooking time
depends on the amount) until you
see it colouring slightly; prepare the
meat and place it in the boiling water;
continue cooking without letting it
come off the boil.
Check the cooking with a probe or a
toothpick, drain the meat and wrap
it in a piece of cloth. Cover it in stock
and leave to cool. Of course, you can
also use the cooking stock although
it is less tasty, skim of the impurities
and fat.

ROAST PORK

INGREDIENTS FOR **4** PEOPLE

2 kg raw capocollo
FOR THE BRINE
3 litres water
300 g fine salt
For the dressing after cooking:
1 tbsp extra virgin olive oil
2 sprigs fresh rosemary
Fine salt to taste

METHOD

Debone the pork capocollo.
Make the brine by mixing the water
and salt in a container.
Use a skewer or needle to make holes in
the meat, so the brine can penetrate well.
Leave the meat to macerate in the
brine for 5 days in the refrigerator,
covered with foil.
After this time, drain the meat from
the brine.
Place the product directly on the
oven shelf with a baking tray with litle
water in it underneath to collect the
fat, cook it in a preheated oven at 85°
C for about 4 hours.
When ready, remove the meat from
the oven and season it while hot with
a tablespoon of olive oil, salt and
fresh rosemary.
Then wrap the meat very tightly in a
sheet of aluminium foil and a sheet of
plastic wrap, so as to make it a sort of
second skin. Let it cool.
When you want to use it, unwrap the
meat and slice thinly.

SHORT CRUST PASTRY

INGREDIENTS

600 g "00" flour
250 g room temperature butter
160 g sugar
4 egg yolks
2 whole eggs
4 g baking powder
½ grated lemon

METHOD

Put the flour on a surface and add the
butter in small pieces.
Knead until you obtain a crumbly
dough.
Add sugar, baking powder and lemon
zest.
Make sure it is all incorporated well.
Add the eggs and mix quickly to
obtain the final pastry.
Keep in the refrigerator covered with
plastic wrap.

PASTRY CREAM

INGREDIENTS

1 l milk
8 egg yolks
220 g caster sugar
75 g corn starch
¼ vanilla stick
1 lemon

METHOD

Leave the lemon peel and vanilla to infuse in the milk for one hour.
Heat the milk, bring almost to the boil.
Separately, mix the egg yolks with the sugar, add the corn starch and stir.
Remove the lemon and vanilla from the milk.
Add the hot milk to the egg mixture gently mixing with a whisk.
Boil it again on a low heat.
Put the cream in a container and let it cool in a pan covered with parchment paper.

SPONGE CAKE

INGREDIENTS

10 eggs
250 g sugar
250 g "00" flour
Pinch of fine salt
1 lemon

METHOD

Whip the eggs in a bowl with the sugar, salt and grated lemon peel.
The preparation will be ready when lifting the whisk, the mixture "writes" on the surface without sinking immediately.
Add very gently to the mixture the sifted flour, stirring with movements from top to bottom, otherwise the preparation will deflate.
Pour the mixture into a buttered and floured baking tin.
Bake at 180° C for 25 minutes.
After baking the cake it must be inverted on a wire rack to cool quickly on both sides.

CHOUX PASTRY

INGREDIENTS

½ l water
200 g butter
5 g salt
350 g "00" flour
8 eggs

METHOD

Heat the water in a saucepan with
the butter and salt; when the butter
is melted and the water boiling, add
the flour.
Stir rapidly, and in order to form a
homogeneous and uniform mixture
similar to "polenta", when it comes off
well from the bottom, remove it from
the heat.
Put in a bowl and allow it to cool.
Stir in the eggs one at a time; work
the dough energetically until it is
elastic.

INDEX

MEAT, FISH & MORE

DESSERT

BASIC RECIPES